THE TINY POTTY TRAINING BOOK

A **simple** guide for non-coercive **potty training**

by Andrea Olson, M.A.

To my diaper-free family:
David, Kaiva, Isadora, and Cooper

TABLE OF CONTENTS

THE PURPOSE OF THIS BOOK

Hello parent. Whether you're a mom, a dad, or a caregiver, welcome.

I'm Andrea and I teach parents how to go diaper free, which means "free from dependence upon diapers." I never imagined this would become my primary occupation, but I embrace it. I feel like an emissary of potty wisdom. We've lost the potty wisdom in our culture in 2 short generations. I'm here to help anyone who wants a life without diapers.

I used to only work with parents of babies 0-18 months, but I found out over the long years of teaching infant pottying that many parents didn't find me until their babies were well past 18 months of age.

This book is the next natural step from my work in the gentle infant potty training method, elimination communication. The potty training method in this book is equally gentle and honors your child's communication about when he needs to go.

Since writing my first book on EC, I've expanded my offerings to include you. And you, my friend, deserve this information more than anyone. When we get honest, really honest, we all agree that depending on diapers through ages 2 and 3 is a drag. Diapers suck, but what's a parent to do?

You see, we are in a predicament these days. Since the advent of the disposable diaper in 1959, the average potty training age has DOUBLED.

You will not find a lot of history and philosophy in this book until far after the "how-to" part. That's because this book is simple. I get to the point. I'm known for that.

But here's a quick look at where we've been:

THE HISTORY OF POTTY TRAINING AGE

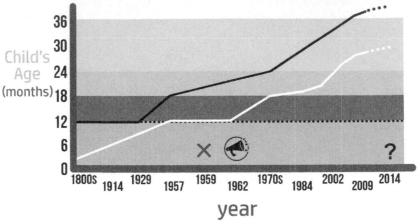

year

We're going to potty learn, potty teach, whatever you want to call it, the way grandma and great-grandma did. Quickly, easily, and gently while honoring our children in the process.

So, in this book, that's my aim. I intend to make this simple for you to do.

I have read practically every book on this subject and have digested it, tossed out the negative, superfluous, and asinine information that you don't need, and organized the remainder into **an actionable plan**.

What is left is only the good stuff of the toilet training community blended seamlessly with my knowledge of pottying infants.

By the way, I have my Master's degree in Psychology. I've worked with children and adults and a whole array of issues. You are, in that respect, in good hands.

I've also got lots of experience helping 1,000s of parents worldwide go diaper free with EC. So, in that respect, I hope you also feel safe in my capable hands.

And I train coaches worldwide to further this message.

Any age: you can go diaper free and free yourself from exclusive dependence upon diapers.

Now for your pep talk. Do not skip this part. It is 100% required prior to starting potty training.

Flip the page....

THE TINY POTTY TRAINING BOOK

THE PEP TALK

Hi. You are awesome for being here. Seriously! Taking the bull by the horns, no matter the age of your toddler. I commend you.

You are gentle, you are compassionate, you put your child first above anything in your life. **You are seriously awesome and I want to support you in completing this task with confidence and gusto.**

This can't be easy for you, especially if you have attempted potty training before. But don't worry. Pretend like I'm your wise Grandmother who knows just the thing to cure your ail.

You know your child best, and I want you to use that knowledge during this process. This book is full of *suggestions*. I want you to read it and adapt it to your own child and find your own way *with your unique child*.

I'm genuinely excited to help you with this parental Rite of Passage. Because it is one. A rite is generally a challenge that passes quite quickly once you surrender to the process and lean in on your inner (or outer) guide. And you come out the other end saying, "Now, that wasn't so bad!"

And, rites require wise guidance and full commitment.

You are supported!

You are reading this book because you want to potty train at some point, whether today or in the future when *you* (not your child) are ready.

All you need is:

- Permission to begin (and train)
- To feel ready, yourself
- A clear plan

You want to potty train without damaging your child, without harming her in any way.

You want to help her feel self-sufficient and supported in learning this new skill.

You want her to be honored in the process. You want to do this gently, yet effectively.

You want to listen to *his or her needs* and to also get your needs met as a parent.

You may not have any clue as to *how* to do this. And that's okay!

PERMISSION TO BEGIN (AND TRAIN)

I hereby give you permission to begin at whatever age your toddler is, particularly 18 months and over. (Under 18 months? My book on elimination communication is for 0-18 month babies. Read that, too, and decide whether to do EC, or potty training, or a blend of both. Plenty of my EC clients have used potty training prior to 18 months with much success. Your choice.) Historically and geographically, your child is *capable* now. More on that in a sec.

And by the way, TRAINING is not a bad word. Think of it as training to run a 5K, or training to become a chef, or training on your first day working at the local donut shop.

We are born knowing *how* to pee. We are not born knowing the socially acceptable *place* to put it. We need to learn *where* to put our pee. We need on-the-job training.

So, training = good.

TO FEEL READY, YOURSELF

I encourage you to honestly assess whether *you* feel *ready* to do this, as the parent or caregiver in this situation. If you don't, no worries…by reading this, perhaps you will be gently nudged over that edge into being the "ready" parent.

And, when are we EVER really, truly 100% ready for anything (um, like having kids!?). *There is never a "good" time for anything, when you think about it.*

Here are some questions you can consider, followed by my thoughts on each:

1. Do you have about a week to dedicate to this process (at least 3 days for the beginning part)?
2. Do you have a strong desire to have your child out of diapers?
3. Do you believe it is *possible* for your child to be potty trained at this age? (Keep reading for the section on Doubts.)
4. Are you *afraid* of your child, his tantrums, her moods, etc?
5. Can you 100% commit to this right now, knowing that I'm going to hold your hand and walk you through it?
6. Can you follow through and not revert to daytime diapers once you've begun?
7. Are you ready for your "baby" to grow up into a little kid?

Let me explain some of the above....

Time. If you can make time, make it. This is such an important step in your child's life. You'd be amazed at how quickly you can clear your schedule if someone in your family becomes sick or needs you desperately. Let's prioritize this.

Desire. If you love your diapers (particularly those of us who use cloth, and all of us who love the convenience of diapers – myself included), zoom out and take a look at how you *really* feel about your child using them as a portable potty. She's carrying her waste in a plastic, gel-filled bag. He is sitting in his poop or pee for any number of minutes at a time. Do you still *love* those diapers? Yes they are convenient...but what is your child's true experience? How badly do you want this? How much does she deserve this?

Possibilities. Do you doubt this is possible? Doubt is a bit dangerous here. If you feel doubt, your child will feel doubt. If you second-guess whether it's the "right time" to potty train, your child will also second-guess it. If you are not sure you're doing the right thing and give up halfway in, your child will also give up halfway in. If you're only doing this because of outward pressure, but you actually aren't confident it will work, your child won't feel confident either. *But do not fret!* We'll cover doubt more in a second and nip that one in the bud.

Fear. It's okay to be afraid of your child...notice it, admit it, talk to someone about it. Then change it. If your child is in control of you, you are in for quite a trip when said child

7

becomes a teenager. It is time to be the parent, parents. Step it up, figure out which boundaries *you* value most, and consistently, with your partner's help (if any), reinforce those boundaries. It is good for your child, good for you, and good for your relationship. Your child does not feel safe when you let him be in control and make you afraid. Your child feels *safe* when you tell him what's right, what's wrong, and what is acceptable in your family (or not). We will also cover this some more later.

Commitment. Commitment is key. Usually we don't commit because we are afraid of the unknown. I invite you take a leap into the dark…knowing that you have a guide in me and this book.

Follow-through. Being steadfast in giving up diapers is also key. Wearing diapers while learning about the potty is counterproductive. I invite you to take the plunge, follow the plan in this book to the "t," and TRUST in this process.

Millions of people…in fact, everyone you know…have been potty trained over the millennia. The key is to not make diapers an option. To follow through. You can do it! Just think *if all of a sudden diapers were not commercially available…what would you do?* Exactly.

Letting baby grow up. Your baby is no longer a baby. I know you know that, but I need to say it out loud. At 18 months and over, we are now working with a full-blown, magnificent toddler. Babying your toddler isn't going to support her highest goals of this stage and age. Help him move into being the toddler he wants to be. He's so ready to do big kid stuff…and to be independent as much as possible, with you in the shadows, there to support.

So those are my thoughts on the questions I asked you earlier. Just think about them and get really clear. And then *you* are ready, my dear.

I am 100% certain YOU are going to do the best YOU can with what you're about to learn.

This is kind of like your first birth may have been for you. We all get through it…somehow…and there is only one way through it…and that way is THROUGH.

Potty training with a great midwife, a cheerleader, a coach, on board can also make for an easier experience. I am here with you every step of the way.

You can do it. Especially with...

A CLEAR PLAN

Precisely the focus of this book: a clear plan for potty training. *(A little sneak peek of what you're gonna learn...)*

One clear plan. There is nothing worse than muddling your mind (and your confidence) with too many disparate messages about a subject.

If you go on Facebook or ask your mothers' group for advice about potty training, you will get about fifty different opinions.

All of these opinions are valid, were right for that parent, and worked for him or her beautifully, but stack them all up and you may feel doubtful, confused, and probably very overwhelmed.

The plan in this book is clear and forthright. I aim to simplify and only share what you should do, no more no less.

I hope you will read this and use it as a guidebook, and only insert those additional things (or take some of these instructions and chuck them) based on your own intuitive sense. Your inner guide is more "right" than I am about your baby, so if something in this book doesn't work for you, or needs an additional ingredient, feel free to customize it to your liking. **You know your child best.**

And...don't inundate the plan and your intuition with 100 other friends' advice and intuition. Just keep it simple. You and me and your intuition.

Before we get started...we should clear up a few things to set you up for the MOST success in this endeavor. These next two sections should leave you feeling encouraged and positive about potty training now.

Here we go....

HIDDEN DOUBTS AND FEARS

You may (or may not) have some hidden doubt inside that could derail your potty training endeavors. Specifically, if you have doubt about whether it's the right time, what exactly you're supposed to do, or whether your child is truly "ready," then you will waver on your commitment and everything will become harder.

Trust me. If you're not clear, sure, or committed, your child will be unclear, unsure, and lax about potty training. You see where I'm going with this.

And, since our society encourages you to wait until your child is absolutely "ready," when something isn't awesome, you will say, "See, I knew it, he wasn't ready yet." (Or you will hear your MIL's voice in your head, saying the same thing.) When, in reality, with just 10% more commitment and clarity, you would have been done with the whole process.

Our society supports our giving up (that means we'll buy more diapers, too!), and waiting til they're "more ready" and "even more ready." **It is an easy out**, which most parents gladly take...but what we didn't know is that the way *through* is *so* within reach when we give up.

It's like transition during birth. We all want to drop out of the childbirth process at this point and let someone else do it. But...transition is the time when the baby's about to crown. Just a few more moments and we'll be done.

Another analogy…it's like stopping 10 feet below the summit and turning around, because you can't see it, and it's just too hard. **If you just walk 10 more feet and *trust*, you have climbed the mountain.**

So, my goal is to pulverize any lingering doubt through this pep talk, and the rest of this book. Because you don't need it. Doubt just muddles everything. :) Let's leave that at the door.

Starting with the….

"READINESS" QUIZ

Sorry. There is no readiness quiz in this book.
If your child is 18 months or older, he or she is *already*
100% "ready" to be potty trained.
That's it.

(And if your child is less than 18 months and you, the parent, are ready to potty train, your child is "ready," too. 18 months is a division I've personally made between my two books – it is based on the scientific research that long-term repetitive memory becomes fully developed between 14-18 months of age. But it is not set in stone.)

So how can I be so sure? No quiz, no assessment, no complex criteria before we begin?

Nope. **I will allow the statistics to speak for themselves, both historically and geographically:**

"92% of children in 1957 were toilet trained by 18 months"
(NY Times, 1999).

"98 percent of children are completely daytime independent by age 4"
(NY Times, 1999).

So, the potty training age has more than doubled in just 60 years. Okay.

As for present-day geography:

"More than 50% of children around the world are toilet trained at about 1 year of age"
(Contemporary Pediatrics, 2004).

"The current average age of potty training completion in the US is 35 months for girls, 39 months for boys." (Ambulatory Pediatrics Journal, 2001).

Are our children that physiologically different from what they were 50 years ago? Also, how could children in other countries, in today's world, be potty trained in 1/3 of the time as in the US, for example, if children across the board are not deemed "ready" until 2 or 3 years old?

History and geography both show that "readiness" doesn't matter. Children are clearly *capable* at much younger ages than we have been led to believe.

You have full permission to potty train at your child's current age, wherever you are today, whether you see markers of "readiness" or not. Readiness is a myth created by diaper companies in 1962, promoted by T. Berry Brazelton (head of the Pampers Institute), and is a phenomenon of only the past 60 years.

"Waiting for readiness" isn't a statement of scientific fact, nor is it accurate historically or geographically. Babies are even born capable and I see babies in my work all the time who take an active part in using the potty as early as birth…including my own two children who were finished with diapers at 9.5 and 13 months.

I'll go into much more detail about all of this in the Background Info section at the end of this book. For now, it's important to know that your child is "capable" now, which is a lot different from "ready." History shows she's capable now. Present-day geography shows he's capable now.

No prob to potty train at the age your child is now. No quizzes necessary.

Full permission granted.

Now let's take a quick look at *how*.

QUICK AND GENTLE

We are going to potty train like grandma did…quick and gentle. Take the diapers off, teach the appropriate things, encourage our kids, and never look back (or go back to diapers).

To address a misconception in our current parenting culture, regarding potty training, **gentle does *not* mean gradual (nor does it mean "casual" or "child-led").**

Every awesome parent I know who constantly tries to do the right thing and become the best parent possible, who is parenting in a gentle, patient, receptive way, automatically assumes that child-led and gradual equals gentle.

I want to honor this wonderful quality in you, and in myself for I am the same as you, and to let you in on a little secret: *The psychology of a toddler requires different.*

Turns out that **clear, firm boundaries** and **direct, simple instructions** cause less confusion and more pride for our little darlings at these ages.

And, on that note, **firm does not equal harmful.** Firm simply means "clear, steadfast, and consistent."

To match a toddler's need for mastery and hunger for knowledge we must create a special kind of environment, one in which the toddler feels *safe, capable, empowered, and honored.* An environment where the toddler thrives.

Therefore, gentle in this case is clear, steadfast, and quick. **Like ripping off a Band-Aid instead of peeling it back slowly.** Which is less painful?

So, I want you to take a second to digest this very important point. Gentle is firm. Firm is gentle. Clarity is freeing. Freedom is found in clear boundaries.

Please do not be "casual" about potty training and allow it to drag on for months and months and months. There is no need for this, as you will see.

You will have the *same* challenges and the *same* successes over the course of 10 months as you will in 10 days.

This is why I did abrupt weaning instead of gradual weaning with my son when he turned 2. My ambivalence about breastfeeding began at 17 months and caused him to feel anxious and nurse more often, with more fervor (which caused me more ambivalence). When I finally made a clear, empowered decision about weaning, the anxiety disappeared and my son happily came along. No tears at all.

Cultures all over the world do abrupt weaning at 2 or 3 years old, commonly held as a rite of passage. It is known to be the "gentle" thing to do. Toddlers' minds don't see things like we do. Turns out, quick and clear is very gentle, and very common in no-nonsense, intact cultures.

If you are like me and you used Attachment Parenting techniques with your baby (babywearing, breastfeeding on demand, cosleeping, bonding at birth, etc.), then when your baby turned into a toddler you likely felt a jolt of reality.

The toddler who replaced your baby needs a different sort of handling. He is on the fast track to learning how to be a human grown-up in this world. He does this best when you actively guide the ship, teach, share knowledge and abilities, and provide clear boundaries.

The toddler does not do well with the hyper- responsiveness and lack of parent-set boundaries found in AP. Some things require a parent to step it up a bit and be a strong facilitator or guide.

This is exactly the case with toilet learning.

On the other side of the same coin, **let's not be boot- camp-rushed** about potty training. Please do not expect it to take exactly 3 days, or 5 days, or 7, and feel like a failure when you don't do it that quickly.

Let's not compare ourselves with other parents, or our children with other children. (Which means you can't post this on Facebook until you've finished the whole process, k?)

Every child is different, and every child will take a different amount of time to reach all of the steps we're going to take.

However, my point is to not drag it out because you think that is "gentler"…ripping the Band-Aid off is gentler than slowly peeling it back.

Potty training generally takes between 3 days and 1 month. Rarely is it faster or slower than that if you are clear and confident…and committed. If you *expect* that it will work, it will. If you are doubtful or hesitant, it will take longer.

I hope that you feel encouraged, brave, and excited about completing this journey together.

Remember what to do if you get stuck: listen to your inner guide and do what feels right in your gut and your heart. Not what's in your head or what you've "heard"…but your own *deeper* wisdom. It's in there. I know it. Just get quiet and listen for it. It'll help you.

You can also hop onto our peer support group once you've activated your Readers' Upgrade at godiaperfree.com/ptupgrade. Sometimes bouncing things off other parents works wonders…and everyone here has read this book, so we're all on the same page.

On the next page I'll share with you the 10 Ways of Being that I suggest for your potty training time.

After that, we will dive right into the training bit.

THE 10 WAYS OF BEING

The following will help you get into the right mindset for this whole process and method.

1. **Be physical** – in this method, we are teaching by physical demonstration and moving your child to the potty, by helping every pee go in the potty. Telling is not enough…*physically* guiding her is the key in the first phase of potty training.
2. **Be consistent** – children learn by repetition, so you must be consistent in your teaching. Keep your energy up and get some support so you can lean on others in other areas of your life for a few days.
3. **Be steadfast** – start as you mean to go on. Be committed and (in a good way) ruthless. This is your chance to show your child how to commit to something and follow through, to not waver, to not give in or back off. If your mind is not fully made up on whether it's right to potty train at this time, or in this way, your child will respond by not fully taking to potty training. Make up your mind and be steadfast with your decision. Follow through. You can do it.
4. **Be kind** – there is no room for coercion, meanness, anger, or punishment in potty training. This is a normal bodily function and we are simply teaching *where* it now goes. We do this with kindness and respect. Of course, we all get frustrated. Acknowledge it, take a deep breath, and carry on. (And, be kind to yourself! You deserve it.)
5. **Be clear** – there is also no room for ambiguity or doubt. When you are very clear, and consistent, your child eventually gets that you are serious and follows in suit. I've taught elimination *communication* for years now, and it's so important to clearly communicate to your child. Again, if you become fuzzy, notice that, take a deep breath, and move forward with a clear direction.
6. **Be short-winded** – when you over-talk, your child may perceive you as fearful and lacking confidence. Sometimes

we parents are genuinely trying to "deeply" teach something, but our over-talking prevents our children from (a) being able to listen and

(b) being able to integrate it through their own self- talk. Be brief and short-winded with your teaching, using simple instructions and brief feedback where needed. Then move on to the next thing.

7. **Be patient** – the learning curve is *not* linear. It is a big ole happy mess. So, please be patient with yourself and your baby. You were patient when she learned to walk or use a spoon...so use that skill now.

8. **Be positive** – not that it's going to be a wholly positive experience, but what I mean here is to *accentuate* the positive. Praise the child for *doing* a good job (not for *being* good, but for having *done* a good job). I used to not advise praise, but I am all for it now. "You did it! I am so proud" is a great form of praise. Not rewards, not stickers, not treats...those externally motivate. I am talking about expressing your approval for when things go right. When things go wrong, clean it up and make a brief statement of the correct action, then move on. You can even say, "No, pee goes in the potty" to show your disapproval of that action. My point here is to *focus on* the positive so that every little success will build, and will help motivate the both of you.

9. **Be non-coercive** – We are not using force, rewards, M&M's, sticker charts, or anything else pressuring. We *are* working at a swift pace, but we are not forcing the process and using external reward systems to bribe our kids in the process. If you've already begun using rewards, stop now and, if asked, say, "We aren't doing that anymore." You don't need to explain yourself.

    Rewards cause power struggles in potty training, bottom line.

10. **Be united** – If you have a spouse or partner, it is very helpful if you are both on the same page about potty training. If you aren't, your child will sense it and will exploit it. If your partner is open to reading this book, it'll put you on the same page. If not, give him or her the

abbreviated version, and if your partner isn't interested in the actual potty training at all, enlist him or her in doing things around the house, cooking meals, etc., while *you* do the potty training. If you have a daycare or caregiver, or if Grandma watches the kids sometimes, please prepare them. Tell them you're doing it, at the very least, and see the Troubleshooting section for more information on "daycares" and the part on "what to say to a naysayer" for more support in uniting your caregiving team.

Your demeanor and patience absolutely affect the potty training process. If you are stressed, it will be stressed. If you are wishy-washy, your child will be wishy-washy about using the potty. If you are ambiguous, your child's level of success will be up and down. If you are verbose, you will show fear and weakness.

For example, I personally tend toward "stressed" (I am Type A, for sure), and so I am constantly noticing that and then regulating my stress level by taking deep breaths. We all have our tendencies. We all have to *stretch* in potty training.

It is the greatest challenge…the greatest honor…to have to rise to the occasion and grow up in little ways during this process (ways in which we've always wanted to grow).

No pressure. Let's work on *being* these wonderful things while in the process of *doing* potty training.

If you slip with any of the above (you ARE human, aren't you?), simply *notice that* and then make an effort to switch back into it. These are moving targets and we can only do our best given our situations…so no hard feelings if you're not perfect (um, who is?). Just strive as much as you can, and understand *why* we're doing each of these things.

They all help.

Now on to the potty training plan….

THE POTTY TRAINING PLAN

Let's get right into the nitty-gritty. Here is what we're going to do:

- **Prep Step:** Ease In (optional)
- **Phase 1:** The Potty Training Experience
- **Phase 2:** Ongoing Independence
- **Phase 3:** Nighttime & Naptime

As I said in the last section, you know your baby best.

Do try to stick with the plan, but if pieces of it need to be modified for your particular baby, based on your own intuition and your knowledge of him or her, go forth and modify.

If you aren't sure whether you should modify any of these steps, just go ahead and use the following plan exactly as written. Trust the process. It is tried and true.

You know your child best, and I want you to use that during this process. This book is full of *suggestions*. I want you to read it and adapt it to your own child and find your own unique way *with your unique child*.

For those of us who are more visual learners, here is an illustration to get a grasp of the big picture of our potty training plan:

A NOTE ON PHASE LENGTH

The potty training Phases vary in length. In other words, we are not looking at exactly one day per Phase, nor are we looking at any particular length of time for each Phase.

You may take a week on one, a day on the next, and another three days on the next.

I will list some recommended timeframes in each of the following Phases, however, I want you to use the *expected outcomes* listed at each Phase to know it's time to move to the next.

When you hit an outcome, time to move on.
Go as quickly or as slowly as it seems reasonable.

A NOTE ON RUSHING

Know also that any *rushing* of the process is what will complicate it. You can encourage and be steadfast and clear...and still not put undue pressure on your child or yourself to complete each Phase earlier than is possible.

Pressure is not the same thing as moving things along, encouragement, and moving forward.

Pressure is what happens when you hope for something *else*, ignoring reality, and you push, push, push to make "that other ideal thing" happen *now*.

Moving things along at a proper quip is different.

Encouraging and moving forward is also very different. We want forward movement and progress, and we can stay focused on that and be patient with the process at the same time.

This note is not meant to encourage you to take it slow, easy, or lax. Quite the contrary. You can move forward at quite a healthy pace and not rush the process while doing so.

I hope you see the difference. Forward movement?

Great! Rushing before the outcomes of each Phase are met? Not advised.

Now on to the optional Prep Step....

PREP STEP: EASE IN (OPTIONAL)

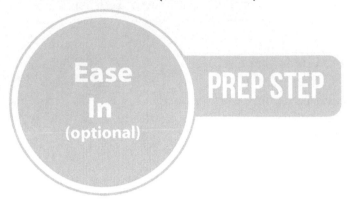

Welcome to potty training! This first step is optional and will help some of you ease out of the diaper habit before potty training officially begins. Read it through and, if it makes sense to you, do it first.

The outcomes we're looking for in this step, at which time you are welcome to move on, is some sense of an introduction to catching pees and/or sitting on the potty at set times, and some self-awareness training for your child to feel the cause-and-effect he'll learn during diaper-free time. Our goal is to feel like we've "eased-in," both parent and child, for about a week, not much more please.

So, how to do it?

Over the course of one week, give or take a few days depending on how you feel about things, I invite you to do two things:

1. **Ease in with easy catches for one week.**
   a. *Morning pee.* Sit your child on the potty first thing in the morning, whether she has a dry diaper upon waking or a soaked one. Sit on your toilet alongside her and do your morning pee at the same time. She doesn't have to pee for this to count. It's just practice.
   b. *At every diaper change.* Sit your child on the potty before putting on a new diaper.
   c. *Before or after a bath.*
   d. *For poops,* if you know the signs.

2. **Daily diaper-free time.** For about 30 minutes to an hour per day, have some diaper-free time with your child. This could mean going outdoors with him naked from the waist down, or it could mean her wearing underwear inside the house, or just pants, or if you have non-carpeted areas, naked from the waist down indoors. The point is to help him see what it feels like to have *no diaper on* for about an hour per day, for about a week. **Warning:** do not over-do naked time, as too much of it tends to teach children to pee on the floor wherever, whenever. A "potty trained while naked" child is not truly potty trained.

3. **Schedule your Potty Training Experience (Phase 1)** for a precise time in the near future, say in a week after you've eased in. Clear out about 3-4 days from your usual scheduled commitments (I know you've always wanted to do this anyway!!) and set up support for other children or housework/meals, or to just plain help you, that you might need.

These three things will help you both ease into what it's like to have no diapers in the picture and will prepare you for the next phase.

If you feel inclined to do so, ease in gradually, but do not spend more than a week or two on this step. With much younger children, more than a week is acceptable, but with older children, limit this stage. The sooner you move on to Phase 1, the sooner your child will know exactly what the goal is with this whole potty training thing.

And, again, if this Prep Step isn't feeling right for you, I encourage you to skip it. Most parents won't need to do it, but some will want to do it for one reason or another. Follow your gut.

The next phase is the most important teaching and learning part of this process. And it can be the most challenging...and rewarding!!

Let me walk you through The Potty Training Experience now....

PHASE 1: THE POTTY TRAINING EXPERIENCE

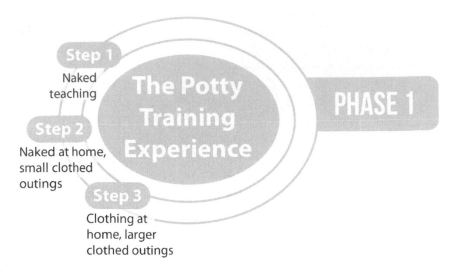

The potty training experience is all about teaching and learning. These days are the heart of potty training...most important in getting you over the "hump." This is not a "boot camp" and, although there are 3 Steps, it is not necessarily going to be 3 *days* long.

The goals for this phase are twofold:

1. **Learning** *when* your child needs to pee.
2. **Modeling** *where* the pee goes, and how to get to the potty.

Learning and modeling. Pretty simple.

This Phase will get you and your child over the initial "hump," which is the gateway to potty independence. **Once you both round this corner with some concentrated teaching and learning time (anywhere from 3-10 days), you will be finished with daytime potty training.** From there it will be all about wrapping up any loose ends and establishing long-term, positive potty habits within your family

TIME LENGTH OF PHASE 1

Just a reminder: this Phase could take you three days, it could take you one day, or it could take you ten. It probably won't take more than 10 days, in my experience, to reach the goals of this Phase. 7 days is average.

OUTCOMES OF PHASE 1

We want to know when we can move on to the next phase of potty training. These are called "outcomes." The outcomes for Phase 1 are:

1. You've learned *when* your child needs to go, which I call the "4 Roads to Potty Time." This includes knowing:
    a. your child's **peepee dance** (signals that she needs to go)
    b. your child's **potty patterns** (natural timing and rhythm of her elimination)
    c. when your family's **transition times** are (common times when most children need to or should go, based on convenient transition times)
    d. what your own **potty intuition** feels/sounds/ looks like (you've noticed that you "knew" or "know" when your child needs to go).
2. Your child has learned *where* the pee and poo goes, based on physically transporting her at every elimination event. She knows that pee goes in the potty now. She knows how to *get to* the potty. She knows how to *sit on* the potty. Clothing manipulation is not a marker of success here. Neither is wiping. But he "gets" that the pee/poo goes in the potty and can get there himself or with your assistance. Things have "clicked" with him. She has gone from no clue –> oops, I peed –> I am peeing right now –> I need to pee. Any progression along this timeline *is* progress and means things are clicking.
3. Your child is *wearing clothing* (naked time has served its purpose) and things are also "clicking" when she's clothed. This can be pants-only (commando), undies and pants, or some other combination of clothing.

4. <u>You both </u>are able to go on diaper-free outings together, and feel a budding confidence with these outings.

When you've achieved all of the above *outcomes*, you are finished with Phase 1 and can move on to Phase 2.

Now... let's get into the details of what you will do together during this time.

WHAT TO WEAR

Step 1: The dress code for Step 1 of this Phase is a short- or long-sleeved t-shirt and no pants or underwear, no trainers nor diapers. Bottomless. Naked from the waist down. All day long (except for naps...we will cover that soon). You can add legwarmers and/or socks if you prefer.

If it is winter or you live in a colder climate, turn up that heat or use a space heater. It's only going to be a day or two of naked-bottomed, on average.

Steps 2 & 3: The dress code for Step 2 is the same as Step 1 while at home. During Step 2, and during all of Step 3, dress your child in a shorter short- or long-sleeved tshirt that doesn't go too far below the belly button, pants only (which we will call *commando*) or undies and pants. If you prefer to use cotton trainers at this point, you may do so *only if* the trainers cause *more* success and do not hinder the process. (PullUps are *diapers* and are simply unacceptable for waking-time, daytime training.)

Phase 1, Step 1: Naked Teaching at Home

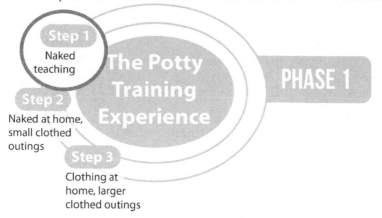

A quick note: You may want to give a few extra juice boxes to your child today, especially if you know you've got a camel who can drink a lot and hold it a long time. If you never give juice boxes, give them today and then never again. You can alternatively feed watermelon and salty pretzels to increase the number of pees for just today. Your call. Point is…**if you find you need more pees for more practice, at any point,** it's fine to augment the diet just for today, in support of this goal.

Okay…now on to what to do!

Step 1 Summary

- ✓ give extra fluids if needed
- ✓ no more daytime diapers, ever
- ✓ tell her what's happening today
- ✓ no distractions (cell, computer, visitors)
- ✓ no outings
- ✓ move her to potty every time she starts to pee or poo, catching at least a drop each time
- ✓ learn the 4 roads to potty time
- ✓ assess your progress and either repeat or go on to Step 2

You will take the diapers off in the morning and say, "You're a big girl/boy now and you will not be wearing diapers anymore." You can totally be excited!

You will then throw them away. If he's old enough, have him throw them away. Throw a whole package away, and the one she was wearing.

Tell her something to the effect of, "Today you are going to learn how to use the potty. From now on all of your pee and poo will go in the potty. You're a big girl now and you're going to use the potty like _____ (name of older kid she knows, or 'daddy' or 'mommy') __ and wear big girl undies from now on. Today we're gonna learn how. It'll be fun."

And then have the morning pee. Close the bathroom door with both of you in it. Sit on yours while she sits on hers. This is what we do in the morning. If she refuses, no worries. She'll have plenty of practice time today where you will *transport* her to the potty each and every time she *begins* to go. More on that in a sec....

You can put the mini potty in the living room or play room with you, or you can use a toilet seat reducer or mini potty in your bathroom. At this point it doesn't really matter where the potty is. Eventually it will be in the bathroom, but for now, we want it as close as possible so there is more chance of catching some of it throughout the day.

You will turn OFF your cellphone, smart phone, tablet, computer, Facebook, and put away your books, magazines, TV remote...every single distraction.

We are reverting to life in the 50's, y'all. Please delete all distractions from your life during the whole of Phase 1, especially this Step 1.

Then you will go through your normal day of playing together with *no outings* (just for today, or another day too if you choose...more on that later).

I know, it can be quite maddening. But take this as an opportunity to *really* connect with your child. Have games to play together, fun things to eat like watermelon or cantaloupe (which encourage more pee), special drinks like juice or milk, and lots of water breaks.

You are going to do something really wild: **you're going to pretend like you're not paying attention to when she pees, but you're going to be so attentive that you don't miss a single one**. Do not make it obvious.

It's like *ninja hovering*. She shouldn't even know you've noticed.

Every single time he begins to pee, you will calmly transport him (lift him up off the ground and onto the potty or into the bathroom) onto the potty and say "potty." Even if you've only gotten one drop in (and a trail of drops behind you), it counts!

It is essential to *only* put her on the potty DURING a pee or poo. Putting her on the potty at random times throughout the day *teaches nothing*.

Remember when we said, "Be physical"? The *physical* act of getting on the potty only *while* eliminating is what teaches. You can *talk about it* til you're blue in the face. But *actually* demonstrating it through the body itself? THAT is what teaches this.

And the repetition of it (all day long today) is what reinforces this.

I am not exaggerating when I say you've got to be on her, on him, noticing his or her every move, all day long. Exhausting? Yes! Rewarding? Absolutely.

Do – not – miss – a – beat.

(Remember, you will only have to do this for a day or two...
it's not forever, just til it clicks. So give it your all.)

With poos, you may get some forewarning. Great! If you already know when it's about to happen, transport him then. If you want to wait til it starts (or it just sneaks up on you), then transport during.

Also during this time you can do some low-key demonstrations of how to get to the potty and sit on it. Make up a dance or a little jingle to go along with it.

My son and I always sang, "Run, run, run to the potty!

Now back, back, squat on the pot."

Demonstrate sitting on this day or do it the week before or some time after if necessary, but definitely physically get in there. Remember, "Be physical"? This is also part of that.

If there is a slightly older, potty trained child in your neighborhood or family, please have him or her demonstrate for your toddler how to mount the potty. Worst case, YouTube is a good place to see kids sitting on potties, but remember…do not get distracted by the computer, or by the small visitor.

LEARNING THE 4 ROADS TO POTTY TIME

In this first step of potty training, during naked time, you are going to learn what I call "The 4 Roads to Potty Time."

These are the four ways you're going to know your child needs to potty.

Learn them all, as they will each tell you when it's time to *prompt* (more on this later). If you're terrible at one or two of them, you'll simply rely on the other 2 or 3 and everything will work out fine until independence.

The 4 Roads to Potty Time include:

1. **Your Child's Signals.** What little signals or indications, via body language, words, or noises, does your child give before she pees?

We can call this a "peepee dance" or your child's "signals."

Notice what you see, if anything, and either write it down or make a mental note of it.

If you don't see anything, look harder. It may be very subtle, energetic even, such as the vibe in the room changing. This is why it's important to not have any distractions like the telephone or Facebook or an actual book during this learning stage.

Here is a list of the most common signals, or peepee dances, for the 18 month and up crowd.

POSSIBLE SIGNALS

- crying
- sudden fussiness or agitation
- discomfort
- grabbing crotch, genitals, diaper, tummy, chest, or underpants
- looking at you with a distressed or concerned face
- getting still
- sudden hyperactivity
- becoming antsy
- passing gas (may indicate pee or poo or both)
- emulating the peeing noise (psss or raspberries)
- walking to the bathroom
- running to you and/or tugging at you out of nowhere
- pointing at or hitting the toilet or potty
- trying to escape the baby carrier
- feet pushing against you, arching back, bouncing, or squeezing thighs in the carrier
- trying to escape the stroller, carseat, or high chair
- stopping eating during a meal (though he's only just begun and isn't finished yet)
- bearing down
- grunting

- hiding as if to go poop
- playing by herself all of a sudden
- holding on to something and "assuming the position" for poop
- popping off the breast while feeding
- squeezing thighs together tightly while in your arms or on the ground
- phantom pee (feels like you've been peed on but you're dry)
- yelling out *pee, potty, or poop* (or trying to say any of the words you're using)
- staring off into the distance (deer in headlights)
- peenie-weenie (partial erection for boys indicating pee is coming)
- squatting while concentrating or looking at you

2. **Your Child's Timing.** What potty pattern do you see? Pay attention after mealtime (or a big drink) and after waking: how much time passes before your child pees or poos?

   If you like logging things, use a log. If not, make a mental note. For an 18 month old it may be every 45 minutes or every hour. For a 28 month old it may be every one and a half or 2 hours. Your child is unique…what is her natural elimination timing or rhythm? Learn that now.

NATURAL TIMING

Patterns unique to your child, based on:

- Amount of time after waking
- Amount of time after mealtime/giving water
- And the spacing thereafter.

3. **Transition Times.** Many common times exist when most children need to go, or when we need them to. For now I just want you to become familiar with them. In the next step (Step 2, outings) you will practice integrating these transition times into your daily life.

Establish these routines to help your child remember to use the toilet. Reminding them through these routines and rituals, and prompting at these times, will help you avoid more wet pants.

Here is a list of common transition times when offering the potty may make sense to you.

TRANSITION TIMES

- Whenever you or a sibling goes pee
- Before leaving the house
- Upon arrival somewhere
- Before shopping or an activity
- Upon waking from sleep
- Before or after a bath
- After (or sometimes during) a meal
- At a rest stop on a road trip
- After missing a pee or poo, in case there is more
- During a diaper change (if you are easing into the process) or a clothing change
- After taking her *out* of anything she's been in for a while (carrier, stroller, carseat, high chair, etc.)
- Before putting her *into* anything he'll be in for a while (carrier, stroller, carseat, high chair, etc.)

4. **Your Potty Intuition.** All parents have potty intuition, it's just more prominent in some of us than in others. Perhaps your husband is more keen, or your wife is the potty pro. Maybe big brother always knows when your toddler needs to go, or Grandma always nails it.

Here are some examples of how intuition strikes us.

(Do not get this confused with *potty paranoia*...your child will tell you if that's what you're hearing [like, *lay off mom*], and if you're hearing intuition, you'll know because your teamwork has resulted in potty success.)

INTUITION

- You have a funny feeling that your kid needs to go
- The word *pee, poo, or potty* crosses your mind
- You suddenly imagine your child needing to pee
- You suddenly have to pee, yourself
- You smell poo or pee (even though she is dry)
- You have a vivid thought or insistence that you are *certain* he needs to pee, or that he can't *possibly* need to pee *again*
- You experience a second random potty thought
- You swear you just got peed on (feels like it, but she hasn't peed on you at all – *phantom pee*)

So that's it for what I call "The 4 Roads to Potty Time," which you're learning in this Phase.

The desired outcomes of Phase 1, Step 1?

You've learned the 4 Roads...and...something has "clicked" and you feel your child is ready to either wear clothing half the time or full time.

What does "clicking" look like? See if there is any type of "Oh, I've peed!" or "My, I'm peeing!" registering across his face. <u>Any</u> type of hiding it from you, upset that they're wet or soiled, feeling sorry for having done it, or not liking how it feels (yucky!) all count as "clicking."

Remember, the timeline is going from no clue –> oops, I peed –> I am peeing right now –> I need to pee. Any progression along this timeline *is* progress and means things are clicking. So long as you are not stuck at "no clue," you may move on to Step 2.

If at the end of this first day you do not feel that she understands, things aren't clicking into place, or you feel that you need another practice day, extend Step 1 to a second day, and a third day if it feels right.

This first step of Phase 1 can last anywhere from 1-3 days. Again, add more days if you see it fit, but likely your child is ready to move on to clothing and outings by day 2 or 3. Let's talk more about what I just said.

How many naked days to do?

Keep doing the Step 1 naked learning/teaching days until something inside your child has "clicked" into place. When she has an accident, she reacts negatively or aversive toward it. When she pees on the potty, she is content or even happy about it. Something has "clicked."

A second day? If things haven't clicked on the first day of Phase 1, do a second day of *naked* teaching/learning. Keep doing naked days until things click, exactly as described above, not missing a beat, or a pee. It can be exhausting, but your hard work will pay off. It will not last forever.

You may alternatively want to move forward to Phase 1, Step 2, and do a hybrid day or two on the second or third day(s). This is basically half naked, half clothed. We will get to that or you can skip ahead now.

Taking care of YOU during the potty training experience

If you aren't okay, your child won't be okay. That is across the board in parenting, and although I know you *know* this already, I am going to have to insist that you are taking care of yourself during these very intense days.

Get a good night's sleep after the first, second, and third days. Eat throughout the day (have your partner or potty training buddy cook for you or order in for you). Have a beer or a glass of that nice wine at the end of the day, once your child is in bed. (Don't overdo it...a hangover wouldn't exactly be ideal!)

And make sure your child gets a good night's sleep, too, so you are both on the same, rested wavelength come morning.

Do not schedule ANYTHING during these potty training days. Remember? Be focused. If there is nowhere to rush off to, there will be no "rush" in the process that can pressure the whole process.

Enjoy not having to do anything, or be anywhere, for a few days. Freedom! It makes most of us feel terrible, but it's so important for the potty training to get done, without a rush to get on to our vacation, holiday, or back to school or work.

NAPS AND NIGHTTIME IN ALL OF PHASE 1

During this first day or two, you may do one of two things.

First, you may ditch diapers for nap, nighttime, and daytime <u>all at once</u>. If we're talking about clarity and direction, ditching all diapers all at once is both a BOLD move and a CLEAR one.

Prepare yourself with the tools in the Supply List section if you need some ideas for extra bed protection.

Read the Phase 3 instructions for Nighttime and Naptime *now* and do daytime and nighttime/naptime training *simultaneously*.

We don't need your child stark naked for naps...clothing is fine...but sometimes underwear and trainers feel as tight and familiar as a diaper. You may want to go commando here, too (more in a sec).

If you choose to potty train day and night all at the same time, begin to dress him in cloth training pants and wool soaker shorts for naps, and protect your mattress just in case.

You may also choose to go completely naked for naps, or dress your child commando (no undies, just loose-fitting pants), as you will soon do in the daytime. Or, in colder weather, put your child in footed one-piece fleece pajamas with no underwear or clothing other than the pj's. Naked inside. This is the opposite of what he's used to and he will understand by trial and error what is now expected of him.

Second option: you can do nighttime and naptime training 2-3 weeks later (after coming to success with daytime training). Some parents like to focus on daytime only for a while, master that, and then move on to nighttime.

If that sounds good to you, great! See the Phase 3 instructions for Nighttime and Naptime potty training at that time (or read it now so you know what to expect).

If you choose this second way, putting nighttime training on hold for a few weeks, then say to your child at naptime or bedtime, "You're going to wear a diaper while you sleep because you are still learning." Your child will understand. Don't overtalk it, just be clear and specific.

It is totally fine to separate day from night in potty training. It really depends on *you and your parental energy/patience levels*, not your child's readiness. Remember? No readiness quiz here either.

Use your best judgment and consult with your partner or other support person for his or her opinion.

PHASE 1, STEP 2: NAKED AT HOME, SMALL CLOTHED OUTINGS

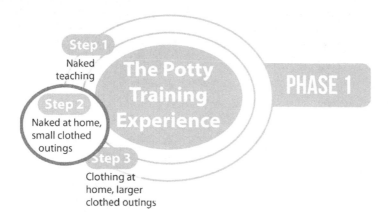

Like I said in Phase 1, Step 1, 1-3 days of naked teaching is the average…and permission granted to go the whole 3 *naked* if you haven't seen a subtle "click" in your kiddo's awareness yet.

In this here Step 2, you will do one or a few *hybrid* days where you are doing half naked and half clothing.

If you guys did great in Step 1, feel free to skip this step and the hybrid days and go straight to Phase 1, Step 3 where you'll use clothing both at home and on outings.

Step 2 Summary
✓ still no more awake-time diapers
✓ child is naked at home, you are prompting
✓ catch a pee in the potty, then…
✓ leave the house on a small outing with just pants (commando), or undies and pants, right after catching the pee
✓ come home and do naked again
✓ catch a pee and immediately leave the house in clothing again

---

In hybrid, you will do outings *in between catching pees*. This looks like: **have your child naked, be totally aware of him and/or prompt and get a big pee in the potty, then do your outing, then come back and go naked again, repeat, repeat, repeat**.

Hybrid day(s) help your child feel successful by letting him be naked while at home (easier for him), catching a pee (success), and then doing an outing with pants-only on, to show himself that he can do that, too (success again).

Once you return home from your 15 minute outing, you will return to naked time to build more tiny successes onto those.

In order to move on to Step 3, you need to make it easy for her to feel accomplished (and help her feel okay with wearing clothing in potty training). Tiny little "wins" will have her thinking, *Hey, I am getting some of this! I feel confident!*

And with more of these wins building a foundation of confidence underneath her, she will feel more encouraged and confident when you both move on to Step 3.

Bottom line: if you want to take advantage of a few more teaching days, which can often help a child with whom it's not yet "clicked," you can do another naked or hybrid day or days, or both, your choice.

To make it even simpler, here's an example of one way to move through the entire Phase 1:

Naked -> naked -> hybrid -> hybrid -> outings -> Phase 2
(little click)   (major click) (Step 2)

And another example:
Naked   ->   hybrid   -> outings   -> Phase 2
(little click)   (major click)   (Step 2)

And a final example:
Naked -> outings -> Phase 2
(clicks)   (Step 2)

So let's now talk about Step 2's shorter, clothed outings.

INTEGRATING OUTINGS

During Step 2, you are going to do four or five 15- minute outings.

Examples include walking around the block with the stroller or carrier, going in the car to the corner store, or a quick jaunt to something very nearby.

Please keep them to 15 minutes, each, at the most. Dress your child either commando (pants only with no underwear) or in underwear, with or without training pants on top, and pants. Just don't use a diaper.

This day is (and following days are) meant to build your confidence. The outcome or goal: **confidence in getting out of the house, integrating potty routines (transition times) into your overall schedule, and continued moving- to-the-potty training while you're home**.

This is the time to put what you learned in Phase 1, Step 1, about *transition times*, into play. During this step, you are going to start lifelong rituals and routines of going to the bathroom at certain times throughout the day.

In the future you will want to offer the potty prior to going on an outing, and upon arriving back home afterward, and in Step 2 you're going to learn how to do that. Also in the future, I highly recommend you catch a pee before leaving, so if, for a little while, you need to wait to leave until that catch is made, so be it. You'll also learn that here.

This way when you're out and about you can have confidence in the timing you already learned (he just went, so you have 40 minutes until he pees again, leaving plenty of time for a 15-30 minute outing).

PROMPTING IN STEPS 2 AND 3

During Step 2 you will begin to prompt your child to go to the bathroom. When one of The 4 Roads to Potty Time happens, you will prompt. Generally, when you see a peepee dance (body language or she says "pee"), you know it's time (it's been however long it usually is for him between pees), you are in between activities or about to have a meal, or your intuition says it's time, you will prompt your child to go to the potty.

This is (almost) never a question. It is always a kind, gentle, and clearly stated comment:

"It's time to pee."

"You're grabbing your peenie…time to potty." "You're doing that peepee dance…let's go."

"Let's go put your pee in the potty before we go on a walk."

You will not *ask* your child if she needs to potty, but you will *tell, state,* and/or *guide* her to the potty.

One exception: *if your toddler says "yes" when she means yes, and "no" when she means no, take advantage of that and ask her if she needs to potty (then trust her reply).* I realize not all toddlers use "no" all the time when they mean "yes" or "maybe," but in my experience, most *do*.

PHASE 1, STEP 3: CLOTHING AT HOME, LARGER CLOTHED OUTINGS

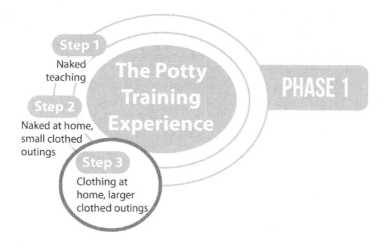

In this step you will begin using clothing *at home*.

When you are finished reaching the outcomes of learning The 4 Roads to Potty Time AND your child is aware of *where* the pee goes and is capable of movement *to* the potty, you are ready to stop *naked* training and move on to *clothed* training. (You've met the past 2 Steps' outcomes.)

Step 3 Summary

✓ no more naked time

✓ longer outings

✓ practice using transition times to potty your child before leaving, upon arriving, and when you go

✓ practice pottying in public restrooms

✓ use either commando (pants only) or undies and pants

✓ still keep an eye on your child all day, no distractions, and prompt when it's time to potty (based on the 4 roads to potty time you learned earlier)

Some of you inserted Step 2, which we just covered, in between naked and clothed training which is kind of a half and half deal – naked at home and clothed on small outings.

Either way, we are all now on Step 3, which features clothing at home and longer clothed outings. Yay!

Why clothing *at home*? You see, we wear clothing in the Western world, and a potty-trained-while-naked child is not truly potty trained.

Begin with underwear and pants (see my Supply List for where to find small enough underwear for your tot), and if you notice that your child pees right through them over and over again, go ahead and switch to commando, which is elasticized pants with *no* underwear or training pants beneath. (See "Pee Issues" in the Troubleshooting section for more info on this.)

You may use training pants instead of underwear on outings, or just underwear, or just commando.

You will need to see what works best right now for your child. This will probably change in the future.

Most parents will find that commando, right now, is MAGIC. Using "just pants" or shorts, with no undergarments, for 2-3 weeks is *different enough* from wearing diapers that children stop peeing in them. And it feels gross to pee in commando clothing. So, if you find that pee is still going in pants, you will want to go commando for a few weeks, then switch back to undies full-time.

Another note, training pants may feel like diapers as well (the tightness and absorption). Use them if you wish, but I truly believe they are best used as extra protection *on outings* (and during naptime when you've done Phase 3 of training – nights and naps), not as everyday clothing during the wrapping up of potty training.

What to do while at home all day. You are still 100% ON IT (which you won't be in another few weeks…but today, you are). While you're at home, you will work together in getting to the bathroom and on the potty on time. You will follow The 4 Roads to Potty Time, which you learned earlier, and upon any of the 4 indicators (peepee dance, natural timing, transition time, or your intuition), you will prompt (or remind) your child to go to the potty and put her pee in it.

You will continue your day without cell or computer distractions, but you're going to go on longer, clothed outings every few hours today.

More on prompting in Step 3. We went over this in Step 2, but for those of you who skipped that step, here again are my thoughts on prompting.

Generally, when you see a peepee dance (body language or she says "pee"), you know it's time (it's been however long it usually is for him between pees), you're in between activities, or your intuition says it's time, you will prompt your child to go to the potty.

This is (almost) never a question. It is always a kind, gentle, and clearly stated comment:

"It's time to pee."

"You're grabbing your peenie…time to potty." "You're doing that peepee dance…let's go."

"Let's go put your pee in the potty before we go on a walk." (when outings come into the picture)

You will not *ask* your child if she needs to potty, but you will *tell, state,* and/or *guide* her to the potty.

One exception: *if your toddler says "yes" when she means yes, and "no" when she means no, take advantage of that and ask her if she needs to potty (then trust her reply).* I realize not all toddlers use "no" all the time when they mean "yes" or "maybe," but in my experience, most *do.*

Now let's discuss these Step 3, longer, clothed outings!

During Step 3, you will expand your outings to 30 minutes at a time.

Once you've reached confidence with these, you are clear to do 1 hour (or more) outings.

Remember, your schedule is still clear. You are still not allowing distractions such as phone calls, computers, Facebook, or even reading actual books or magazines. You are doing the basics. Potty training like grandma did. Yes?

Yes.

So, by this Step, you are still ON IT. But now your child is clothed, you guys are working together (prompting/signaling), and you are venturing out together, more and more each day.

How to potty on outings. When on these outings, always locate the nearest bathroom upon arriving somewhere. If you're going out in nature, bring the Potette Plus to use on the trail, or on the side of the road if needed. When your child signals a need to go, pull over and find a restroom or use the mini potty in your car or the Potette Plus to potty her.

To reiterate, during these outings **you will practice pottying at Transition Times as part of the big picture**.

You will also use the *other* 3 Roads to Potty Time....

So, here are the 4 again. You'll either notice a peepee dance, know that it's her natural time to need to pee (a certain amount of time has passed), it will be a good time to go (before leaving the store, for example, or upon arriving before a shop), or your intuition will indicate that it's time to pee.

And on these outings, especially when you get to the longer ones, you will *practice* being in tune with your child's potty needs just as you are *already* in tune with her need to eat, drink, and sleep.

In potty training, we are only expanding our awareness to include pottying...we already know our children so deeply. Just zoom out a tiny bit and here we are.

The outcome of this step is comfort with wearing clothing...that the clothing feels different than the diapers did, and that wearing clothing (the right combination of it) *enhances* the potty training experience and *encourages* independence. **And we are also aiming for successful outings.**

HOW TO KNOW PHASE 1, THE POTTY TRAINING EXPERIENCE, IS DONE

Once you've gotten over the hump of Phase 1, The Potty Training Experience, you'll have achieved the following outcomes (to reiterate from earlier):

1. you know when your child needs to go...The 4 Roads to Potty Time (peepee dance, natural timing, transition times, and your own intuition)
2. your child knows where and when to go potty, how to get there and how to sit on it...things have "clicked" for him or her

3. your child is aware of when he needs to go beforehand, at least most of the time
4. your child is now wearing clothing (commando or undies and pants) and things are "clicking" while clothed, too
5. you are able to do diaper-free outings together and your child has had potty success outside of the home.

All the above means you are done with Phase 1 and ready to move on to Phase 2.

In Phase 2 we will look at the continued learning required after you've gotten over the "hump" of Phase 1. **You have "potty trained" and now you're wrapping up all the loose ends, if any, to promote full potty independence.** (Ummm…congrats!)

Here we go….

PHASE 2: ONGOING INDEPENDENCE

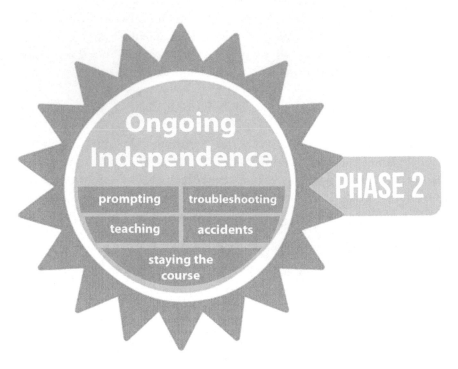

Congratulations! You're done with the potty training bit.

Now it's time to solidify these good potty habits, work on any weaker or lingering parts of the process, and continue handing off the baton to the point where your child is 100% potty independent. **This is Phase 2.**

(You may call your child "potty trained" at this point, if you wish. Once they've done Phase 1, it's done. Hooray!

Now it's just a matter of reinforcement and encouraging full independence. Staying the course. Showing your child you mean business and this is the new norm.)

Ongoing Independence is basically day-to-day life post-potty-training. It is a time to continue staying the course. It is not a time to EVER go back to diapers (if they're no longer available, there is no struggle and there is no crutch). It is not a time to give up if things regress all of a sudden (we stay the

48

course). It is a time to continue demonstrating, teaching, and working on any loose ends.

Remember our talk about *capability*? If you see any backsliding at all, it's part of the process and you should stay the course. Be steadfast. Your child *is* capable. Stay the course.

Your child is past Phase 1 and has thus "rounded the corner." From here, it is all about establishing lifelong habits and full-on independence.

She has already demonstrated understanding and capability. Now we show her we're serious and make this a NORMAL part of day-to-day life…supporting "do it myself" fully and completely.

The outcomes we want in Phase 2 are:

1. *full potty independence*, and
2. *good lifelong potty habits.*

Again, your child is already "potty trained."
Now we're gonna seal the deal, completely.
I'm excited for you guys.

The parts of Ongoing Independence. We have a few main ideas here: prompting, troubleshooting, teaching (the learning curve, teaching weaker or lingering parts, placing the building block skills of full potty independence), accidents, and staying the course. Let's begin….

PROMPTING

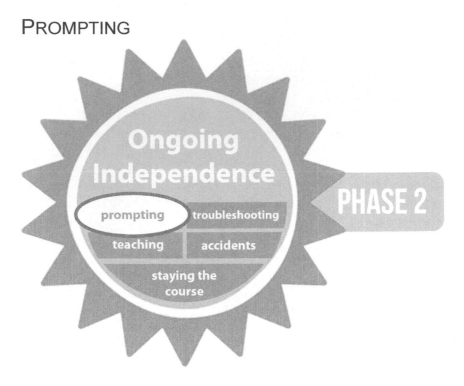

You will probably prompt your child to go to the bathroom through his 18th birthday. It's just part of life. We all need a little reminding every once in a while.

As we mentioned earlier, we don't *ask* if they need to, we make a statement when one of the 4 things that indicate potty time occur. (Eventually, there will be very little prompting and you will hardly have to pay attention...I promise that day will come soon enough!)

Upon completion of Phase 1, it is unrealistic to expect a child to initiate every single potty trip from there on out. She needs reminders, but a certain type of reminder. We will cover that shortly.

But for now, you will likely have to prompt most of the day for a good 2-3 weeks until she gets the hang of it, and thereafter probably once a day, depending on the age of your child.

So, prepare to prompt. It is not a sign that things have gone wrong (neither is the lack of self-initiating)...*it is a natural part of any teaching process*…the guide comes along for a good while *after* the teaching is complete and supports until the student is completely self-sufficient.

A little reminder like "You're dancing around…time to go pee" is always helpful for our little ones who are involved in learning *so much* at these ages. This type of reminder calls your child's attention to his body language and helps him to know, for himself, when it's time to go. "You are grabbing your crotch. Let's go pee."

Remember, you can avoid an automatic "no" response by not *asking* her if she needs to go. **Simply state**, "It is time to go to the toilet" or "It is your turn to use the toilet" or "Time to go pee." Or don't say anything and just hold hands and walk to the bathroom together.

Do not say, "I *think* you might need to go now, let's try," because it shows that you are unsure. Even if you weren't spot-on, show confidence at every turn. It's not about being right or wrong in the end, but in using The 4 Roads to Potty Time to guide you in guiding him to the bathroom until he takes the lead, which won't be long.

Another thing I discourage is "overprompting." This happens when you sit there in front of the potty and say to her, "go peepee, time to go, let's hear your pee, come on now, gotta go so we can get back to playing, go peepee, potty time." Can you tell how that amount of overprompting and overtalking would cause *anyone* to resist what you're trying to get them to do? Be short-winded.

Sometimes overprompting occurs when we don't even realize it. This type of child needs more of a gentle nudge and then a walk-away. Let me explain.

With a child who is older and/or clearly wants more privacy (and, for example, resists and has accidents all of a sudden, for no apparent reason), you'll want to **toss out a prompt** instead of directly prompting.

You will say…*you're squeezing your crotch, time to go pee*…and leave her in the bathroom (with pants already off or pushed down if you are still helping her with those). You then **walk away** and allow her the freedom to do it herself.

If your child is 18-24 months, you can do the **semi- tossed out prompt** by getting him ready to go (pants off), prompting him (which is your recommendation that he goes), and then *ignoring him or turning your back* while you're still in the bathroom, busying yourself with something else. Or you can pretend that you forgot something in the other room and *leave* confidently and come right back. Usually as you slip out of presence, your child will go.

I used to call for the dog to come in when I noticed resistance in my 13 month old yet I knew she needed to pee. She wanted privacy but was a bit too young to just leave at it. So, I called "Ollie!" and pet him and focused on our dog for a little while and she peed or pood every single time with zero fuss *while* I ignored her and tended to the dog.

Another ninja parent move.

The *tossed out* and *semi-tossed out* prompts are super- awesome tools. Use them after it's clicked enough with your child that you are willing to take the risk to leave him to it.

And take the risk! Worst case, you get some pee on the bathroom floor. No biggie.

If your older child *really* wants privacy, close the door and walk away. Nothing terrible will happen. Promise.

For more information on overprompting and its relationship to resistance, please see the "Resistance" section of Troubleshooting in this book. And check out the "Accidents" troubleshooting topic to learn why a sudden onslaught of accidents and resistance actually means your child wants privacy.

TROUBLESHOOTING

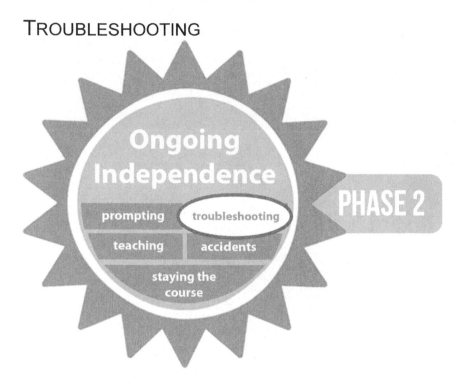

During Ongoing Independence, you are basically going to face any challenge head-on and work to iron out any wrinkles you may face.

You may have none, you may have minor issues, you may have major problems, or, you may have no issues but imagine you do have an issue because it's not all peaches and cream (and you were told there would be peaches and cream).

While I encourage you not to create a problem where there isn't one, I also want you to nip anything *you* deem an issue, in the bud, as immediately as you can.

Please see the Troubleshooting section of this book for answers to the most common questions, and gain access to our peer-based support group for more help at godiaperfree.com/ptupgrade.

TEACHING

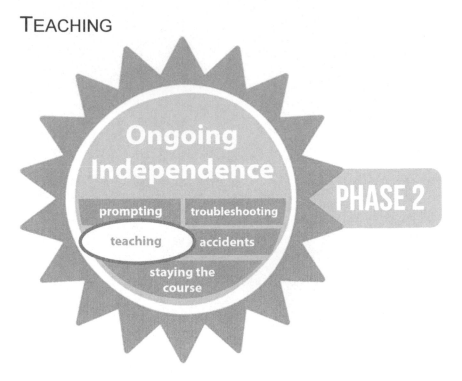

The learning curve. Expect this to look like a nonlinear jumble for a little while. As your child puts all the pieces together, the puzzle will become complete. Just as learning to read can look all askew from our parental points of view, so can learning all the bits of the potty process.

Which leads me to what things to teach, and how, so that full independence happens more easily....

Teaching the weaker or lingering parts. As you get over the first hump of training, you will notice that some things very clearly need to be strengthened. Perhaps it's clothing manipulation. For some children it will be wiping. For others, washing hands. For others, dumping the potty themselves will be the challenge.

Whatever the weaker or lingering part is for your child, during the completion period, you'll be tying up loose ends by teaching some things.

Which brings us to...teaching some primary potty skills!

Teaching the building blocks of independence. The following are skills that build a tower of mastery within your child, like those little wooden alphabet blocks. These are things she may or may not know how to do yet.

Learning (and mastering) them gives your child all of the pieces of the potty puzzle...which is a tremendous gift.

Here are some examples of skills you can teach that will add up to full potty independence in the end:

Pushing down pants. Notice that I did not say "pulling down pants"...<u>pushing</u> is the key here. Have your child grasp her pants and "push" them toward the ground, bending at the knees halfway through.

If you're having trouble with this, start small. Pull your child's pants a little bit and then have him finish. Or pull them down halfway and then have her sit on a small stepstool and ask her to push them the rest of the way off.

Over time, encourage him to do more and more of the pushing himself.

Dressing your child in easy to manipulate clothing will help in this teaching, so if you have some loose elastic- topped pants and maybe undies that are a size bigger, you can use these for a while until your child gets it, then move back into more "fitting" clothing.

Sitting. We went over this in The Potty Training Experience phase but I'll remind you of the main point here: teach by demonstration (you or a small child should sit on the mini potty or seat reducer to demonstrate).

Teach her (1) how to get there and (2) how to mount the potty. Use a song or chant if you wish. "Now run, run, run to the potty, and back, back, squat on the pot." That was ours. Use YouTube if you don't have a willing live model in your neighborhood or home. Grab a neighbor's kid to demonstrate for you, or have a playdate with a slightly older child and ask her to show your kid how to do it. Most older children love teaching young ones the ropes.

Also, normalize sitting on the potty by having an "open door policy" in your own bathroom. Relax your boundaries about bathroom privacy for a little while and let your child see all family members using the bathroom and sitting on the bigger toilets. After she's learned the ropes, you can begin to close the door again.

Wiping. You will not have to teach a boy to wipe his peenie, but you will teach a girl to "blot" her yoni for good hygiene. This is as easy as handing her a small wad of toilet paper and telling her to touch it to herself and then drop it in the bowl. As she becomes more adept, encourage her to wipe from front to back, not back to front, for obvious reasons.

For poop wiping, here is a suggestion: have your child grab two squares of toilet paper and wad them up or fold them, depending on his level of perfectionistic tendencies.

Have her bend over and put the toilet paper in her crevice as far as she can, and see if any poop is on the toilet paper.

If he has ever explored his anus in the bathtub, this should be no problem. If not, help her feel where it is by manually guiding her hand there.

Then, have him repeat the check with a new bit of toilet paper to see if the tp comes out clean or has poop on it still. When there is no longer poop on the tp, it's all done. "Try again until the paper comes out clean and there is no poop on it."

If your child gets frustrated, simply guide her hand and try again, or if you've got a meltdown brewing, ask her to bend over, wipe her yourself, and tell her to check the toilet paper and see if it's clean or dirty. Then, at least there is some learning going on, and try again next time.

You can also gradually introduce wiping by doing it all yourself first while briefly narrating what you're doing, then starting it and having him finish, or having him begin the wiping and you finish it up, and lastly, having him do the whole process.

Throwing the toilet paper in the toilet. Always a fun step!

Unless it's a soiled poopy mess, just fold over the toilet paper after you or she wipes, and say, "Throw it in!" If you are using a mini potty, he can stand up and throw it into the big toilet.

Pulling up pants. This can be a challenging skill for our wee ones. That cute little booty seems to get in the way of getting those pants up and on. It is often helpful to have a full-length mirror in a non-potty-part of your bathroom so your child can see what's going on (I don't recommend placing it in front of the potty, as that may cause distractions, but somewhere else, such as on the wall behind the door or on the door itself).

As I mentioned in the pushing down pants part above, you may want to dress your child in looser elastic-topped pants and perhaps a size up in undies for a couple weeks to help her feel a sense of ease in accomplishing this step. Once it has been mastered, you can revert back to normal-fitting clothing. This is an option only if you need it, as many parents do not see the need to augment clothing for this step.

Focus on this every day for a few minutes, during potty time or at another focused teaching time, and eventually your child will get it.

If the undies are completely off, have your child identify the undies tag and teach her that this part goes in the back. Hold open the waist and show him where the leg holes are.

After she puts her legs into the holes, pull them up to her knees, then ask her to stand and pull them up.

Another recommendation I've read is to have your child pull up the back of the pants with one hand while pulling up the front with the other (instead of having one hand at each side). The hand at the back of the pants will be oriented with her palm facing *away* from her body and grasping the pants while your child stands up from a bent- knee position. The front hand can be positioned comfortably. This should help him get over that rump.

Alternatively, you can pull up the backside of the pants while he pulls up the front, until he gets the hang of the whole thing. Or just help in any way you can.

Don't overthink it, but do teach it over time and encourage her to eventually do it herself.

Dumping the potty. If you're using a mini potty, teach your child how to remove the bowl (if any) or pick the potty up (if it's one piece) and carefully dump the potty in the big toilet. You'd be surprised at what age children are capable of doing this! You can guide her hands at first and "do it together," then work your way toward "you can do it yourself." Kids always show a sense of pride at dumping their own potties and being careful with them.

Flushing. Toddlers love flushing so much that this may not be something you have to teach. Pulling the handle down with two hands is a nice suggestion that makes it a tiny bit easier to flush the toilet. Don't forget to say "bye- bye" to the poop or pee! Then close that lid. Gently.

If your child is afraid of flushing, please see "Fear of flushing" in the Troubleshooting section in this book.

Washing hands. Have a step stool handy that can get your child within reaching distance of the running water. Use whatever soap floats your boat: foaming pumps or colorful bars or something that smells yummy...whatever. The goal for your child is to get that lather going. We want bubbles! A friend of mine either counts with her children or sings the ABCs together every time, to ensure the washing has gone on long enough.

Then rinse, dry hands, and the bathroom routine is done.

The whole routine. Speaking of routines, getting using the potty in the context of a bigger routine is definitely helpful. Do it the same way every time, as our toddlers are big on learning by repetition. Remember all those times you've read the same book, over and over? Or played the same song? Yes, repetition creates mastery...and heaps of pride.

An example routine: run to the potty, flip on the light switch, push down pants, sit on the potty, [tinkle or poo], wipe, put the toilet paper in the toilet, pull up pants, dump the potty (if any), flush the toilet, wash hands, flip off the light switch, back to playtime.

ACCIDENTS

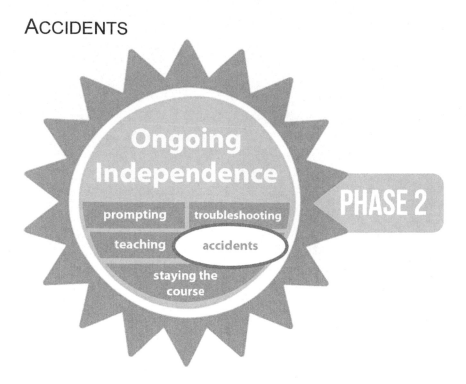

In the Elimination Communication world of training 0- 18 month babies, we don't call accidents *accidents*...we call them *misses*. As in a missed opportunity, or missing the potty, or simply missing a signal (the child or the parent).

I'm fine with using the term *accidents* because it's common language where I live. Yes, to some it implies a mistake, but it's semantics to me. No big deal. For now we will call them wet pants. Dealing with day-to-day wet pants for a little while is somewhat normal after potty training.

Here is some information on how to work with wet pants, followed by information on how to handle a sudden increase in accidents.

One of our Go Diaper Free community members, a Montessori toddler teacher and parenting consultant, wrote a research paper titled *Child Neuropsychiatry: Toileting*. In it she shares the Montessori educator's way of dealing with wet pants in the infant community (or classroom) setting, in which children wear cotton training pants during the 12-18 months of age range, inspiring completion by 18 months.

Here is an excerpt from her paper:

When a child has wet pants, calmly take the child into the bathroom.

- *Remove the wet pants (with her help if possible) and put them in the hamper.*
- *Have the child sit on the toilet. If the child complains, talk matter-of-factly, saying something like, "Let's just see if there is any more urine in your body."*
- *After a brief period, have the child get off the toilet and sit on the bench facing you.*
- *Ask for and expect the child's cooperation in putting clean underpants on. For example, show the child how to find the tag of the underpants, and where to place it. Hold the waistband open and show the child where the leg holes are located. After the child puts her feet in the leg holes, put the pants up to the knees, then ask the child to stand and pull them up. The child can pull up the front while you pull up the back. It is helpful for the child to be able to see himself in a*
- *full-length mirror while pulling up his pants.*
- *Ensure that the child washes his hands thoroughly, emphasizing the bubbles.*
- *Try to change toddlers in the standing position. If the toddler needs to lie down, use a low changing mat or a portable mat hanging on the wall.*

Elizabeth, thank you for the excellent advice from your wisdom and the wonderful Montessori way.

I think the biggest take-away from this advice is **the calm and matter-of-fact tone** she suggests taking with your child upon discovering wet pants. **And I love that Montessori incorporates *teaching*** into every step in order to reap something from the experience.

Sudden accidents about a week into potty training. Normal, normal, normal.

When your child has done great at potty training, gotten over the hump, and you are in Phase 2, Ongoing Independence, it is very common to all of a sudden experience resistance and a sudden increase in accidents.

Your child is asking for you to give her control over the process. You will need to (1) reduce the frequency of your prompting and (2) give her some privacy.

If this happens to you, please read the "Resistance/Sudden increase in accidents" section of the Troubleshooting chapter in this book. This is not something to be alarmed about.

STAYING THE COURSE

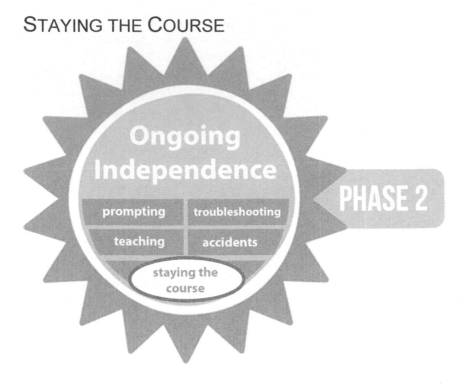

The reason our grandmothers found it so easy to potty train our parents is that **they made the decision and stuck with it**. There would *not* be another diaper to wash. No one was keeping tabs on them via Facebook. There was no competition amongst their mother friends. There simply would *not* be another day of changing diapers. *Period.*

My own mother selected a time in the near future when she'd have her first full week alone with my sister to potty train her...and she never looked back thereafter. She had to work outside of the home before and after potty training, and there *was* no going back. It absolutely had to be a done deal.

I know parts of potty training can be very difficult, and very taxing. However, do not give up. Be encouraged.

During the weeks that follow getting over the hump, just stick to your guns. Do not go back to diapers. Make it very clear that "this is what we do now" and that "all pee goes in the potty now."

The gentlest thing you can do is be clear and confident. And stay the course.

Just stick with it and know that this will all be over soon. The day will come (sooner than you might believe) when you will not have *any* hand in your child's potty business.

And you and your child will be sooo proud!

Til then, be encouraged and stay the course. Millions of parents have trod the path before you. And when you look back someday, this point in time will seem so miniscule and fleeting.

PHASE 3: NIGHTTIME (& NAPTIME)

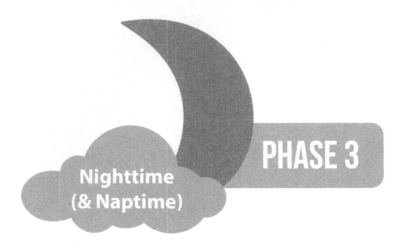

Welcome to the dark side...of the 24 hour period, that is! Whether you are doing this training concurrently with daytime Phase 1 training or you are doing night/nap training separately, as Phase 3, the following is a suggestion of what you can do, step-by-step, to complete this half of the potty training day-night cycle.

For naps, **the outcome** of this phase is that *your child will hold it all nap and wake up dry.*

For nighttime, **the outcomes** of this phase are one of two things:

1. your child will hold it all night and wake up dry, <u>or</u>
2. your child will wake up to ask to pee (or take himself) in the middle of the night or early morning, and return to sleep.

If #2 is your outcome, great! Many of us adults (present company included) can't hold it overnight either. Some adults never pee at night. It just depends. If you are in the #2 boat, over time, #1 will take over for your child as he matures. Eventually, he will be able to hold it all night and wake up dry. For our purposes, #2 is just fine for now.

By the way, it *is* **physiologically possible for a toddler to hold it all night** (we all emit hormones that keep us dry and unsoiled while sleeping), and yet in some cases it must be tackled in stages and learned over time.

She has been wearing diapers during *every* sleeptime until this point. We must have patience while guiding the ship to completion.

You can best support this nighttime and naptime mastery by following the steps in this section.

WHEN TO START NIGHTTIME/NAPTIME TRAINING

Two options:

1. Start either *simultaneously* with Phase 1, Step 1, daytime training, or
2. Start 2-3 weeks *after* daytime potty training, Phase 1, is successful/complete/complete-enough-for-you.

Just decide on one plan of action and carry forth. You'll use the same instructions in either case, which I will now explain.

THE VARIOUS WAYS TO NIGHT/NAP TRAIN

Some suggest waking up your child once or twice each night to pee, some suggest just going for it from the get-go, and others suggest using PullUps until they start coming up dry in the morning.

I am very partial to going for it because I believe our children are *capable* of more than we can imagine. I think waking a child to pee is a personal choice and I wouldn't particularly be up for waking my sleeping child. But it works for many parents. I am not too keen about using PullUps until they start coming up dry. If you are teaching a child to be dry at night, putting her in diapers sends a mixed message and is counterproductive. And PullUps *are* diapers.

However, I also have experience with a wide variety of families and I know that one size does not fit all. Therefore, I'm going to present a few ideas on how to approach nighttime/naptime training.

NAPTIME TRAINING

When you (the parent) are ready to tackle naps, whether simultaneously with Phase 1 daytime training or separately a few weeks later, follow these steps.

Mattress protection. Be sure your mattress is protected…see the Supply List for more information on how to do so.

Essentially, you can either "double-make" the bed with two sets of sheets and a mattress protector in between them, or you can just use one set of sheets with a layer of protection below them, as this is just a nap and your child probably won't return to sleep after peeing in her bed.

Nap dress options. You can go commando with loose-fitting elastic pants and no undies, or use underwear only, or underwear and pants, or underwear with cotton training pants over them for extra protection. Wool soaker shorts can contain a pee accident if you layer them over the undies or training pants (do not dress them in the wool shorts alone…they won't work quite right without something in between to absorb the pee).

Dress your child in whatever works for daytime. If you're new to daytime pottying, use whatever you've been using. If that means having her sleep naked, so be it. Some will have their child nap in the same clothing she was wearing while awake. Some will change him to pajamas.

Some will do naked. Your choice.

Overall, **feel free to adjust the naptime dress code over time to use whatever discourages accidents and encourages dryness.** It is different for every child.

Fluids before nap. Do not give your child a ton of fluids right before naptime. Ensure you are giving her lots of fluids upon waking and throughout the waking hours, but at about *one half hour to one hour before naptime*, start to limit fluids or at least be aware of how much you are giving (so you can adjust them later if need be).

If you give a sip of water before nap, give it in a super tiny cup. This way you can avoid guzzling and a full bladder going into it.

If you're still nursing to sleep or giving your child a bottle to sleep with, I encourage you to consider changing what you're doing. Nursing to sleep is a habit I picked up with my first child. With my second, we use other ways to get our child to sleep. She is a much better sleeper, by the way, and I owe it to our changed ways.

A couple of good resources that helped me do it differently with my second child, and which many in our community have tried, are *BabyWise* (omit the CIO part, please!) and *The Nursing Mother's Guide to Weaning* (which covers weaning for naptime). Your child, at age 18 months or greater, no longer requires nursing to sleep for nutrition, only for comfort. Also, putting a child to sleep with a bottle has been proven to negatively impact dental health.

So, all that to say please consider your options if you're doing either of these heavy fluids prior to naptime, as they will affect how much your child pees (or doesn't) during a nap.

Final pee-pee. Do a matter-of-fact "final pee-pee" before every nap, and make it a ritual. If you have a naptime routine, integrate this as a natural step in the progression to sleep.

Summary. Watch pre-nap fluids, dress appropriately, super tiny sip of water (if any), final peepee…then go for it! If there is no diaper or disposable underpants to pee in, your child will either hold it or wake to pee. Or have an accident once or twice then become encouraged to hold it so she can get some sleep.

Nap accidents. Sometimes the only way to encourage her to hold it is by having an accident or two. They are part of the process, cause and effect if you will. In time, the instincts will take over. Just watch fluids, do a final peepee, and dress him for success.

If you are having a lot of pee accidents at naptime, try having your child sleep naked for a few weeks…it feels the furthest from wearing a diaper. Crank up the heat.

No more nap diapers or PullUps. Lastly, please do not use PullUps and do not revert to diapers at naptime if you can at all help it. Remember the "Be physical" part? That also applies here. If there is not a potty (aka *diaper*) physically attached to them, they must wake to use one *or* hold it til they wake.

Note: If you are getting poops only at naptime (or nighttime) all of a sudden, please see "Poop, at night," in the Troubleshooting section of this book.

NIGHTTIME TRAINING

Night dress options. You can either go for underwear right away or use cotton training pants over underwear, or put wool soaker shorts over one or both. Using two piece pajamas is a good idea if you will be pottying at night.

Commando (or naked) is a perfectly good option if your child needs the exact opposite of a diaper.

One-piece fleece pajamas (completely naked inside), once peed in, feel gross, so if you have a child who needs some creative inspiration to not pee the bed, you can try that. It worked wonders for my son. One pee in those and he would either wake or hold it every night thereafter.

Feel free to adjust the nighttime dress code to whatever encourages the least accidents and the most dryness. It is different for every child.

Protect the mattress. Do this in the same ways as in naptime training, above. You can double-make the bed or have a thick, heavy fleece blanket nearby that you can throw on top of peed-on-sheets and have your child sleep on top of, if necessary. More on that later.

Fluids before bed. Do not give your child a ton of fluids right before bedtime. Ensure you are giving her lots of fluids upon waking from her nap and throughout the waking hours, but at about *one to two hours before bedtime*, start to limit fluids or at least be aware of how much you are giving (so you can adjust them later if need be).

If you give a sip of water before bed, give it in a super tiny cup. This way you can avoid guzzling and a full bladder going into it.

If you're still nursing to sleep or giving your child a bottle to sleep with, I encourage you to consider changing what you're doing. Nursing to sleep is a habit I picked up with my first child. With my second, we use other ways to get our child to sleep. She is a much better sleeper, by the way, and I owe it to our changed ways.

A couple of good resources that helped me do it differently with my second child, and which many in our community have used, are *BabyWise* (minus the CIO part, of course!) and *The Nursing Mother's Guide to Weaning* (which covers weaning for nighttime). Your child, at age 18 months or greater, no longer requires nursing to sleep for nutrition, only for comfort. Also, putting a child to sleep with a bottle has been proven to negatively impact dental health.

So, all that to say please consider your options if you're doing either of these heavy fluids prior to sleeptime, as they will affect how much your child pees (or doesn't) during the night.

Final pee-pee. Do a matter-of-fact "final pee-pee" before every night of sleep, and make it a ritual. If you have a nighttime routine, integrate this as a natural step in the progression to sleep. If your child is closer to 18 months in age, do the final pee-pee as the very last step in the whole nighttime routine, even if it means getting back out of bed after reading a story.

Summary. Watch pre-bedtime fluids, dress appropriately, super tiny sip of water (if any), final peepee...then go for it! If there is no diaper or disposable underpants to pee in, your child will either hold it or wake to pee. Or be encouraged to hold it so she can get some sleep.

No more diapers or PullUps. Please do not use PullUps and do not revert to diapers at night if you can at all help it. Remember the "Be physical" part? That also applies here. If there is not a potty (aka *diaper*) physically attached to them, they must wake to use one *or* hold it til morning.

Here are some more specific guidelines and suggestions. Please choose the ones that resonate most with you, if any:

Story-time reminder. At toddler age, one of the biggest influences on our kids' brains are the characters in their books.

As you're reading his favorite book before bed, mention that, "This boy wakes up when he needs to pee and yells 'Mama, peepee!' Can you yell really loud? Show me how. [He yells loudly.] Great! This boy keeps his pants dry at night. His mama helps him pee, then he goes back to sleep."

And at the end of the book, remind her one more time "Yell 'MAMA, PEEPEE!!' when you need to pee tonight and I'll help you. Keep your bed and your pants dry."

That last mention will keep this top-of-mind and eventually he will tell you every time, or hold it all night long (which are our desired outcomes for Phase 3).

Waking to pee. If you want to know exactly when your child is peeing at night, and to offer the potty then, you will want to wake him to pee. A lot of parents choose to *only* nighttime train in this way. It is your choice. **If you choose this method, please stick with it and see it through.**

Start with a 10pm and a 2am wake-up to see if your child is wet yet or not. Have the potty in her room and make a "pssss" sound while you help her sit on it (probably while she leans on you in sleepy form). Some have their kid pee into a cup while leaning on them (sounds tricky, but it does work). Keep the lights low and if she refuses, simply put her back in her bed and wake her up at the next time (2am).

Adjust these times as you see fit until you hit that magic time when he is wet, then start waking a little before that time and potty then. Set yourself an alarm and commit to doing this each and every night until you reach your goals.

Eventually, you are going to wake her later and later until you have met the normal wake-up time and your child is sleeping through the night dry.

If you aren't into waking a sleeping child, then skip this part.

If you night-nurse. If you know your child has to go or if she has difficulty settling after a nurse, or during a nurse, at night, potty her before or after the nursing session. Have the potty in your room and make a "pssss" sound while you help her sit on it (probably while she leans on you in sleepy form). Keep the lights low and if she refuses, simply put her back to bed. Perhaps try it at a different time next time if it results in an accident: before, instead of after, nursing, or even *during* nursing if you're acrobatically-inclined.

If you night-nurse but you don't want to do it any longer (I have been in your shoes!), please see *The Nursing Mother's Guide to Weaning* book which will help you night- wean with gentleness and clear direction.

If you co-sleep. You have the benefit of *knowing* when your child needs to pee at night. When you feel that uncomfortable wriggle and unrest go ahead and offer the potty in the same way as above in the night-nursing subsection.

Night accident clean-up. Keep an extra pair of pajamas handy <u>and</u> (1) either double-up the bed with a mattress protector beneath each layer of sheets or (2) have a fleece blanket nearby that you can place *over* the wet sheets for your child to continue sleeping on, then clean up in the morning. Do not punish, shame, or scold. No one wants to wet the bed!

Deep sleepers. If your child sleeps so deeply that she can wake up in a bed of wet sheets and pjs and not know that it happened at all, then she is a deep sleeper. Try one of the potty alarms on the market and work your way toward the day when she will wake to pee, or hold it. That day *will* come.

Holding it. It is not harmful for a child to hold the contents of her bladder. If it hurt, she would release her bladder's contents immediately. Our children are the last people who want to cause harm to themselves. They are 100% into self-preservation.

So, do not fret about them holding it all night long.

Physiologically, if it hurts to hold it, it is released. That is the nature of sphincters. Remember childbirth? With or without you, that baby was coming out.

Parental or doctoral fear that holding it will harm our children did not come from science or physiology…so don't sweat it.

Nightlights. Be sure your child can make his or her way to the bathroom or potty at night (some keep the potty in the child's room at night) by installing nightlights at strategic locations.

When bed-wetting is a problem. If your child continues to wet the bed through his 6th or 7th year, seek professional assistance. Otherwise, occasional bed-wetting is currently the norm in our society, so do the best you can to deal with it and teach good potty habits, day and night.

Remember, our goals in this phase are for our children to either (1) hold their pee all night, or (2) wake up and ask to pee (or go by themselves)…or with naptime, to hold their pee all nap long.

When you reach these outcomes, Phase 3 training is complete.

That's all for our potty training journey! Please read the following chapters for more helpful tools and solutions to supplement and support your hard work….

A quick note on how to know your child is FULLY potty independent… 100% DONE

I am consistently asked this question, so here is my answer:

Your child is completely potty *independent* (not potty trained, but independent) **once you no longer think about the potty every single hour**.

During training and the months thereafter, it will be on your mind quite often. Eventually, it just won't be, and you'll be sitting there thinking, "I haven't even *thought* about the potty in hours, or days."

And that, my friend, means potty independence is completely in the bag. Not potty *training*, but potty *independence*, is now complete. Yay you!

SUPPLY LIST

A quick note on the potty environment: keep all of the potty tools easily accessible. Your child needs to be able to reach, or have easy access to, the clean undies, toilet (with a step stool), mini potty, toilet paper, laundry basket, sink, soap, towel, and trash can.

A key to Montessori learning is to have everything at the child's level. This creates an *environment* that is easy for your kid to maneuver *independently*. We want to encourage independence, so setting up the correct environment helps tremendously.

And now for your supply list. I'll start out with an overview list and then share with you more details right after, including where to get the best of these tools.

At the bare minimum, you are going to need:

- A potty or toilet seat reducer
- Elastic-topped pants
- Underwear
- Mattress protector
- Portable potty seat
- Wet/dry bag

Extras include:
- Cloth training pants for outings
- Carseat protector
- Potty cozy
- Space heater
- Sheets, blankets, towels, or yoga mats to protect carpet
- Post-it Notes
- Wool soaker shorts
- Fleece one-piece pajamas (with feet)
- A full-length mirror in the bathroom

Here are my recommendations for these items, based on the experience of my readers (and their babies and toddlers), and my own personal experience with each tool.

POTTY OR TOILET SEAT REDUCER

The best potties on the market include:

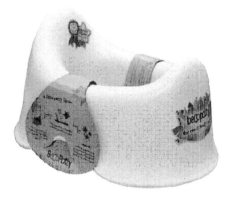

bEcoPotty – a biodegradable potty that is low enough to encourage a deep squat, a position which supports easier elimination and bowel movements. This is a pretty small potty, though, so if you have a larger kid you may want to go with a larger one. Learn more at godiaperfree.com/becopotty.

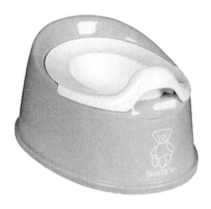

Baby Bjorn Smart Potty (godiaperfree.com/bbsp) or Potty Chair (godiaperfree.com/bbpottychair) – these both have a removable dish in them for easy cleaning. The Smart Potty is simple with no back, and the potty chair has a tallish back to it. It really depends on your baby's preference.

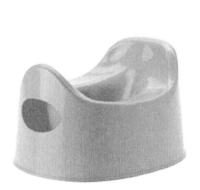
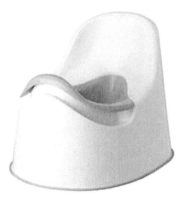

IKEA potties – very affordable, IKEA currently offers two potties and a seat reducer. The smaller one-piece potty is good for the car, while the other model offers a removable dish for ease of cleaning. I have not heard news of the seat reducer and haven't used it myself, but it seems to be well- contoured. Learn more at godiaperfree.com/ikeapotty.

My favorite toilet seat reducers include:

Ginsey padded toilet seat reducer – very affordable and very novel, it is often fun to have your child "go peepee on Dora" or "go peepee on Lightning McQueen"…as these seat reducers feature characters. I am a no-movies-before-2- years-old kind of mother, myself, but it doesn't hurt to use one of these reducers with characters. It personalizes the experience and encourages potty trips to go see their "friends," regardless of whether your child knows the character. These seats are padded and have handles, are very sturdy, and the boy models feature a flexible rubber splash guard that is quite effective. Find one at godiaperfree.com/ginseyreducer.

Bumbo toilet seat reducer – very cushy and supportive for the tinier rears, some children prefer the squishiness. You know if your child is that kind of kiddo. Learn more at godiaperfree.com/bumbo.

Potette Plus – this is an incredibly useful toilet seat reducer because it doubles as a travel potty and mini potty. More on this in the portable potty section below, but for now, know that you can use the Potette Plus at home as well as on-the-go. Find one at godiaperfree.com/potetteplus.

ELASTIC-TOPPED PANTS

In the beginning of training, you will decide whether you want to use underwear, cotton training pants, or go "commando" (just pants alone) for a few weeks. If your child pees straight through undies or trainers without a word edgewise (because they feel snug, like a diaper), you will want to go commando with simple, elastic-topped pants for 2-4 weeks. If your child is fine right away in undies or trainers, you will find it easier to use elastic-topped pants on top of those undies or trainers. Either way, elastic-topped pants are a must. I won't list my favorites here because they are all great in my eyes! And I am a sucker for a good deal, so I get most of mine at consignment shops for $1-2 each.

UNDERWEAR

It has historically been quite impossible to find underwear in the right size for our potty trained little ones, so I started Tiny Undies to fill this need. I offer them in sizes ranging from 6 months to 5T. You can check out all the adorable details at TinyUndies.com. They are affordable and adorable, if I must say so myself.

With Tiny Undies, I specifically wanted to make underwear that are anatomically correct, fitting well underneath the "gut" of the small, growing child, a gut which ebbs and flows as our kids hit their growth spurts. Get chunky, grow taller and slimmer, get chunky again, repeat. The leg holes and rise in 2T/3T underwear are usually giant, resulting in an uncomfortable sag, and the elastic waists are difficult to maneuver. I hope you will find Tiny Undies the perfect solution for your potty training needs. They are offered in unisex, bold colors, sweatshop- free, 100% natural materials.

I can't honestly recommend other underwear because none of them fit all that well. Commercially available undies in size 2T/3T generally fit 3 or 4 year olds. Remember…the national average for potty training in the US is 3 years...so the need for smaller underwear is not that big. (I aim to change that.)

MATTRESS PROTECTOR

Most toddler beds are lined in plastic anyway, so you may not find this necessary, but for those who use organic mattresses or want extra nighttime protection, here are your options:

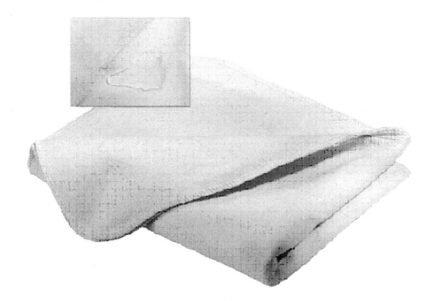

Wool puddle pad – for the most natural sleep and least sweating side-effect, a wool puddle pad is quite awesome. You can either make one yourself out of 100% wool felt found at a fabric store, you can sew together several old wool sweaters and "felt" them in the dryer, or you can purchase a handmade and affordable one at godiaperfree.com/puddlepad from Jenay at Naturally Diaper Free.

100% cotton waterproof mattress pad – Sealy makes one that contains no artificial materials, which will help reduce sweating if you have a plastic-lined mattress underneath. Learn more at godiaperfree.com/sealypad.

By the way...

Never use a PUL-lined (plastic-backed) mattress protector or changing pad underneath a sleeping child. Can you say *sweaty mess*!?

You may also choose to "double-make" the bed by doing a regular sheet set up, covering that with a mattress protector, and covering that with another set of regular sheets.

Or, when you have a nighttime accident, throw a thick fleece blanket over the wet sheets, change your child's pajamas, and put her right back to sleep on top of the fleece blanket.

PORTABLE POTTY SEAT

I have literally tried them all, and the best portable potty seat is, hands-down, the Potette Plus. Not only is it affordable, but it transforms into a mini potty if you must do a road-side pee over grass or concrete, or if you have the biodegradable bags or permanent insert you can use it in your car. This is the only pinch-free public toilet seat reducer I've seen and the fact that it's super-stable helps your child feel right at home…and safe, which is so important when pottying in public. I recommend practicing with this seat at home and your child will willingly use it on outings as well, whether as a mini potty or as a toilet seat reducer. Familiarity is important to most toddlers. Again, learn more about this seat at godiaperfree.com/potetteplus.

WET/DRY BAG

I have found this particular item to be so useful that I made a huge effort to source the best one out there and have it manufactured for my Tiny Undies store (available at TinyUndies.com). The wet-dry bag I sell has two separate zippered pouches...the one in the front is smaller and less waterproof (the "dry" part) and the larger pouch is for the wet stuff.

I stash 2-3 pairs of extra dry undies and pants (and sometimes socks) in the zippered dry pouch of the bag and anytime we have an accident I stick the wet clothes and undies in the zippered wet pouch until I get home. These bags launder very well and hold up to a lot of use, and you can also air-dry between uses. The wet/dry bag essentially replaces your diapers and wipes in your diaper bag (although you may choose to still carry wipes for a while – they always seem to come in handy).

CLOTH TRAINING PANTS FOR OUTINGS

Two choices here, both helpful when layered over undies or used solo under pants when you are on outings and are continuing the training while out of the house.

Priceless!

Note: do NOT use Pull-Ups…they are diapers. You can not toilet train *with* diapers. It is counterproductive.

Your choices:

Tiny Trainers – these are also my invention…a cotton-lined version of my Tiny Undies, great for smaller kiddos and for those who wish to have an anatomically-correct fit.

or…

Gerber cotton training pants – these are pretty large on most smaller kids, but they are good when paired *over* a pair of Tiny Undies for extra protection during outings. Find some at godiaperfree.com/gerber.

CARSEAT PROTECTOR

Since you won't be using diapers on outings anymore once you're through training (and during, for that matter), it's a good idea to have some protection on your carseat.

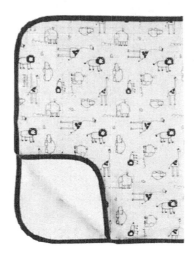

You can either use a Kushies PUL-backed training pad (godiaperfree.com/pads) folded up underneath your child's tush, or grab a Kiddopotamous carseat protector at godiaperfree.com/piddlepad.

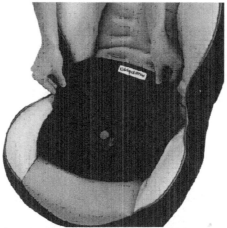

Another option is to use a cotton prefold or burp cloth, or a hand towel.

POTTY COZY

Most kids, babies, and even adults, do not like a cold seat during some seasons, or at all. I highly recommend a cozy if you know your child is sensitive to things like this. You may only find out after trying. With some children a cozy can really help to make the potty "cozier" at the beginning of training. Jenay makes one for practically every potty at godiaperfree.com/pottycozy.

SPACE HEATER

Before making the climate outside or inside your home the prime reason for delaying potty training, consider investing in a simple space heater or cranking up your heat for a few days while you do The Potty Training Experience part of the process. The temporary increase in expense will make all the difference...and remember, your child is *capable* now, so the "cold weather" excuse has now been marked off your list!

SHEETS, BLANKETS, TOWELS, OR YOGA MATS TO PROTECT CARPET

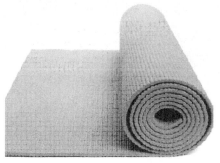

Hit up that thrift store for some old or worn-out sheets, blankets, or towels to throw over your carpet for those training days. Yoga mats can also help. Use something that you don't mind soiling, and something that is practical and large enough to cover the space within which you'll be working.

The stress of possible carpet ruin (especially in a rental) can be a big barrier to your potty training efforts.

POST-IT NOTES

To keep those auto-flushers on public toilets from ruining your child's trust in foreign potties, please bring along a few Post-it Notes in your bag. Stick one on over the sensor prior to using the toilet and you and your child will be happier for it.

WOOL SOAKER SHORTS

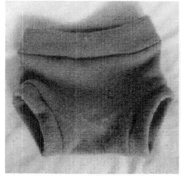

Whether you are switching to underwear or cloth trainers at night, wool soaker shorts are excellent for keeping any wetness off the bed. They are essentially liquid-containing, liquid-repellant "shorts" that are made of breathable and natural felted wool, and they work great for extra night- or naptime protection.

Jenay makes them from reclaimed wool material at her shop (godiaperfree.com/woolsoaker).

FLEECE ONE-PIECE PAJAMAS (WITH FEET)

For a child who wets occasionally at night and might need a little incentive for *not* wetting at night, dress him naked in fleece,

footed, one-piece pajamas. If she pees in these, it will be contained, and honestly, it will feel gross to her. It is likely that nighttime wetting will either be limited or disappear altogether with this extra incentive…if there is nothing to wet *into*, there is more reason to hold it and/or wake to go to the bathroom and then return to sleep.

FULL-LENGTH MIRROR

If you have a full-length mirror in the bathroom, your child can more clearly see herself while learning how to pull up or push down her pants. If it's a distraction, install it on the door, away from the potty, and only use it for the undressing/dressing bit, not the actual pottying part.

THE BACKGROUND STUFF

I'm going to assume that you've picked up this book because you have a hunch that potty training is imminent, or perhaps you have a strong desire to train your child *now*.

Instead of trying to convert you or convince you, I'm going to give you the basics of what you need to know to support the decision you've *already* made.

HISTORY

I just want to share where we have been, and when.

What was the norm, and what major things have helped us veer so far from potty wisdom, as a culture?

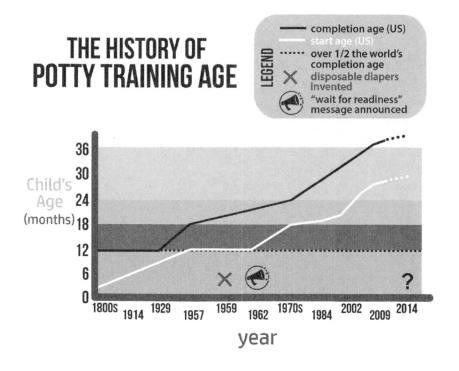

The red "x" on the timeline is the introduction of disposable diapers. The megaphone icon shows where the pediatrician working for the major diaper companies began with his "wait for readiness" campaign (as the chairman of the Pampers Institute, to be specific).

It's pretty clear what has happened over the last 100 years. I'll leave it to you to do the math.

Philosophy

The average potty training age has <u>not</u> doubled because our babies are less and less "ready" for it, or because we've gotten more and more "gentle" with them...but it <u>has</u> doubled because of the convenience of disposable diapers (and the associated marketing efforts of the big diaper companies)...and the mistaken belief that in order to be "gentle" we must "wait til our children show signs of readiness." In other words, it has become unnecessarily long, messy, and drawn out.

Long-term diapering has become our cultural norm in 60 short years. It's just where we're at...no guilt or shame needed. You've got this book in your hands and can tell others the news...and that is great.

Earlier in this book we looked at history and geography to put training into perspective. These next few pages expand on those notions.

We looked first at these historical statistics:

"92% of children in 1957 were toilet trained by 18 months"
(NY Times, 1999).

"98 percent of children are completely daytime independent by age 4"
(NY Times, 1999).

This clearly demonstrates that over the course of 60 years the potty training completion age has grown over 2x. That's a 167% increase, to be specific.

Were children in 1957 very different from the children in 2007? Not likely. Same physiology, same brain function, same general developmental milestones. Over 200,000 years of evolution, 50 years has not changed our children that much.

Let's look at mothers. In 1957 women washed diapers by hand. They were home nearly all the time. There weren't nearly so many distractions or pressures as we have today. Mothers were completely ready to ditch diapers, for sure. So perhaps part of this is the mother's attitude and readiness.

That *has* changed in 60 years.

Other things have changed, too. Nowadays, yes we parents are more busy. Children are overscheduled at age 2. And disposables are more convenient. Those are all givens.

But let's look again at our children, readiness, and bring in the concept of *capability*. This is where it gets interesting.

When we look at our *children's* capability, we see that our children are *capable* of potty training starting at birth, age 12-18 months, 18 months, 24 months…because these ages have been the exact completion ages at various points in recent history. If it *happened*, that means they're *capable*…it is *possible*. **That has not changed.**

I am personally 100% certain of this capability because all of my EC readers of my first book started potty learning between birth and 18 months, especially at the 3-8 month range. From direct experience, I know that *babies* are born ready. They are born *capable*. **They have sphincter control, the ability to communicate their needs, and a desire for cleanliness, from the get-go.**

Your toddler is no different.
(She's just been in diapers longer.)

Therefore, the natural conclusion becomes: whenever the parent is ready, the child is capable. **There is no need to wait for "readiness" or for the child to show an interest.**

The child's *capability* is there, and that capability has not changed over the past 50 years. I hope that makes sense.

That's it for history. Now let's look at present day situations, and geography.

"More than 50% of children around the world are toilet trained at about 1 year of age"

(Contemporary Pediatrics, 2004).

"The current average age of potty training completion in the US is 35 months for girls, 39 months for boys."

(Ambulatory Pediatrics Journal, 2001).

How could children in other countries, in today's world, be potty trained in 1/3 of the time as in the US, for example?

Very simply, we have a predominant message in our society telling us to "wait til they're ready" and "take it slow." You don't want to psychologically damage your baby by starting too soon, or doing it too quickly.

Well, I call that BS.

Add in the disposable diaper phenomenon of the past 60 years (which, yes, has brought with it an incredible amount of freedom and convenience), the fact that late potty training is now the social "norm," and the lack of intact culture to pass on potty wisdom organically from generation to generation, *and you've got a plain mess.*

If we get back to capability, we see that children in Westernized countries are just as *capable* as children in non-Westernized countries. Yes, we use different tools; yes, we have different cultural settings. But...**our children have the *same* physiological capability**.

This is why, in our pep talk earlier in this book, I gave you permission to potty train at the age your child is, today.

I find it so interesting to look at history and geography in order to challenge our own cultures' myths. Let's look at those more deeply....

MYTHS

We've all heard a few ridiculous myths about potty training that have been adopted as "truth" in our culture. The following is a compilation from many of the resources listed at the end of this book along with my thoughts on each.

1. **Children don't have sphincter control until 18-24 months** (say the nursing textbooks in America). Not true. From helping 1,000s of parents learn Elimination Communication over the past several years, we've found from personal experience that sphincter control is present starting at birth to two weeks of age. With practice, sphincter control naturally sustains with age and use. Babies are born with a strong instinct to not soil themselves, their caregivers, or their sleep space…and some level of sphincter control is necessary to physiologically support this instinct.

   Also, remember the rest of the world. Their children all demonstrate sphincter control by completing potty independence between 6-12 months of age. They are not physiologically different from our children.

2. **Early toilet training can psychologically damage a child.** That would mean that throughout the 200,000 years of our current human form, all of the world's children up til about 100 years ago who were potty independent by ages 6-12 months <u>were</u> <u>psychologically damaged</u>. And over ½ the children in the present world must also be psychologically damaged, because they are all trained by 1 year old. Doesn't make a lot of sense.

   When I visited West Africa in 2000, I noticed that in the intact cultures with whom I lived there was an absence of mental disorder. And an absence of diapers.

   This soundbite simply doesn't add up.

   There *was* a brief period of human history where people strapped babies to potty chairs all day long and put suppositories in babies' anuses to get them on a rigid pooping schedule. **That <u>was</u> possibly psychologically damaging.** Toilet training at an age earlier than 3 years old (or using EC)? Not damaging.

Nelson's pediatric reference textbook states: "There is little to indicate that the experiences involved in toilet training of most children are of major psychological consequence" (Lekovic, 2006). So we can all rest easy in that.

3. **Children don't know that they are eliminating.** Jill M. Lekovic shares scientific studies in her book that illustrate direct medical evidence that newborns *know* when they are peeing or pooping, brain studies and all (Lekovic, 2006). My personal experience with EC and teaching EC for very young babies indicates the same. Babies are very aware of it. And, your toddler is still aware of it. Take away that super-wicking diaper and give some opportunities to do otherwise, and that awareness comes right back into play, like a rubber band once pulled. It all comes back. It's instinctual, neurological, and a hard fact that children *do* know when they are eliminating, even after prolonged diapering.

4. **Boys take longer to train than girls.** Some studies have shown boys take longer and some have shown the opposite. The results are not conclusive. The certain fact is that boys and girls are physiologically different. However, different does not mean *takes longer* or *is more difficult to train*. Boys and girls each have their unique qualities, and at this age, are on relatively common ground as far as development goes. This myth can transform into an excuse to drag things out with your son. Boys are actually much more physical than girls (though I've seen some pretty physical girls), so potty training will be more physical than verbal with some boys. See the difference? But gender doesn't dictate outcomes.

For example, my son was out of diapers sooner than my daughter. Yes, the process was different with each of them, but the completion age was not gender-dependent.

5. **Children who train early have more frequent accidents.** There is no correlation between the training method and periods of accidents post- training. I encourage you to see the references section of *Diaper Free Before 3* to find the exact research (Lekovic, 2006). Here, I will respond by saying that, if this were the case, both historically and geographically in today's world we would have a ton of kids with frequent accidents, and that just isn't the reality. And it doesn't make sense that if the muscles are conditioned to hold it and put pee in the potty, at an early age, that that these muscles would be weaker than muscles that were taught this later. The muscles of the earlier trained child would be stronger as a result of more use. The muscles of a later trained child would require more conditioning to catch up.

Earlier trained children do have to urinate more frequently, however, and this is because their bodies, and bladders, are smaller than older children. If the child has not been effectively toilet trained, then of course there will be more accidents, regardless of the age of training. If the parent does not continue to prompt and teach and finish the whole process to independence, of course there will be more accidents, regardless of the age of training. And, lastly, if the child, of any age, is "casually" potty trained, there will probably be more accidents because the child is pretty casual about potty training, herself...regardless of the age of training.

6. **Pee training is easier than poop training.** Children get the sensation to pee or poo and it is one and the same at first (which is why we have boys sit to train...because the sensation for both is so equivalent in the beginning of training). Over time the difference in sensation becomes clearer to our children, and they are able to differentiate between the two urges more distinctly. But most of us pee when we poop, so physiologically, they go together, and the sphincters tend to release together. (We mothers

also poop during birth, to put that point into clearer focus. The sphincters often release at the same time.)

Okay, so then where does this myth come from? Our present-day culture has quite an overall issue with poop training, and a lot of it has to do with parents' personal opinions and comfort level regarding poop. Maybe more substantial is that we are dealing with later and later potty training ages, leaving many children resistant to pooping in the potty because it feels unfamiliar after pooping in a diaper for so many years.

Physiologically and process-wise, pee and poo training are one and the same. Our perspectives about them, personally and culturally, are what differ.

7. **Early training causes constipation and bowel issues.** This is Dr. Hodges' whole platform for selling his book. Dr. Hodges, if you haven't read him yet (I would recommend against it unless you have a 4 year old with constipation issues), works directly with older children who suffer from bowel or bladder complications. He does not work with normal, healthy children, and his research does not apply to them. He insists that waiting *longer* to toilet train will prevent these issues from happening. To the contrary, these things happen *because* parents are waiting *too long*. A ball of poop getting stuck in the colon only happens when training much older children. If you are in this situation, Dr. Hodges can absolutely help you and he's a great resource. For the rest of you, do not worry, and do not let what you have read fool you. Early training *prevents* constipation and bowel issues.

8. **Sitting on the potty randomly, without peeing, is good practice.** Not really. Sitting *during* the act is good practice. Sitting on the potty just to "practice sitting there" is not really productive. Teaching your child how to get to the potty is helpful and necessary, and how to

mount that potty: invaluable. But sitting them there at random times doesn't teach anything. Follow the directions in this book and teach them to sit when they *are* going. This teaches volumes.

Also, do not put the potty out before beginning training to let your child get used to it. It doesn't teach anything. It should come out when training begins, and be used for the purpose for which it was created.

8. **We must wait until our children show signs of potty training readiness or show an interest in the potty.** This is an idea that *probably* had good underlying intentions (ah, except that Pampers funded its spread) but has been recklessly interpreted and applied. Lekovic goes into great detail on this topic in *Diaper-free Before 3*. Unfortunately, this myth does not have a basis in scientific research or factual reality.

You will recall that almost all children were toilet trained by 18 months in 1957. Then, disposable diapers were invented in 1959. They were not well- received, and no good mother would dare put her child in paper diapers, at first anyway. Then in 1962 Brazelton did a research study (Brazelton, 1962), which I've read cover to cover, and concluded that we should wait til our children show signs of "readiness" to begin potty training. However, when you read the study, you see that there is nothing scientifically backing his conclusions. Readiness is merely his opinion. The "findings" were further promoted by Brazelton via his position as a leader in the Pampers Institute, no doubt to encourage parents to use these new disposable diapers. When we look at the order of events, and deeply look at the study itself, we see that readiness is not based in scientific research or factual reality, and a Child-led Approach to Toilet Training, as the study is titled, is merely Brazelton's opinion as well.

The truth of the matter is that when a child is able to walk, a child is also capable to toilet independently...a child is then "ready." There is no "first you reach this milestone, then that, then this one over here, and *then* you can toilet train." Nope. Never has it been that way. Someone *made that up* (the pediatrician who worked for Pampers). Do the math.

If we wait for our children to "show interest in the toilet," it may never happen. Sometimes it happens at 16 months and the parent shrugs it off as "too early" and waits and waits...and the child never shows interest again. Approximately 5% of children self-train (the ones whose parents brag most loudly about it only taking 1 day to train their 3.5 year old), but for most, *we* put them into diapers, and *we* determine *when* to take them out of them. It is our job to be ready, as parents, not our children's job to say they're ready. That's a lot of responsibility that doesn't make a whole lot of sense.

Grandmothers and great-grandmothers, and all of human parents in history, never waited for "readiness" – they expected that when a child began crawling or walking they could also toilet themselves, and they were correct.

9. **It's easier to train a much older child.** It is a shame that this soundbite has become "wisdom" in our current culture. It simply isn't true. After 2 or 2.5 years of age, our children enter a period of asserting independence and saying *no* to most everything – all essential to their separation and development as unique human beings. The older they get, the harder it is to toilet train them. If your own child is not yet fully potty trained and is over 2.5, you'll just need to be that much more stalwart and steadfast in your potty training efforts! Don't fret. But don't wait *any longer*...it does not get easier with age. Power struggles abound (as you know)...and physical issues such as medical constipation and bladder issues are more likely to develop with older, untrained children.

Training as early as possible is much easier for most children (and parent). Historically and geographically, we again see that training between 12-20 months works/worked most fluidly. If you are here at an early age, start now. If you are here at a later age, start now. If you are here pre-18 months, get my other book on Elimination Communication and start that now. If you wish to do EC with a future child, I encourage you to look into it.

Bottom line: this is a myth…start now. And tell your friends.

BENEFITS

The benefits of nipping toilet training in the bud are plenty. Specifically, the benefits of *early* toilet training (starting as young as 18 months) are pretty clear.

Let's take a quick look at these. These are meant to bolster your confidence. Remember, it was only about 60 years ago when almost every child (in the US) was potty trained by 18 months. You, too, can do it, no matter what age over 18 months your child is.

(And with a next child, try Elimination Communication from birth…or potty train right at 18 months with this book. It's great to have options!)

The benefits of both early and completed toilet training include:

- *Finishing earlier.* The earlier you start, the earlier you finish. Every time.
- *Increased self-esteem & dignity.* A child who can do this herself, putting her refuse in the proper place, is going to feel confident, self-respected, self-assured, capable, and proud.
- *Faster body awareness.* The less time spent in diapers, the more quickly children learn their internal "I need to pee" signal.
- *Easier socialization.* There is an inherent sense of shame associated with soiling oneself, and as babies turn into

toddlers, this shame intensifies, interfering with social interactions. A potty-trained child is more able to develop a strong sense of belonging and self esteem in social situations.

- *Positive environmental impact.* The less diapers you throw away, the better. As of 2009 in the US alone, 27.4 *billion* diapers were put in the landfill every year, full of feces, urine, and chemical gels. No disposable diaper, worldwide, has *ever* biodegraded since their invention in 1959. That is some pretty crazy math.

- *Decreased expense.* Diapers are just plain expensive, whether you use cloth or disposables.

- *Assurance of completion.* Most children never voluntarily ask to begin using the toilet. A small percentage will say, "I'm ready" and self-train, and yet other children will never hit that point. When you make a focused effort to toilet train, you assure completion of the process (instead of causing it to drag out).

- *Decreased risk of UTI and accidents.* The sooner and more directly you train and wrap up training, the stronger your child's urinary system will become.

- *Decreased risk of constipation.* The older you train, the more likely it is that your child will have constipation and bowel issues. Train at whatever age your child is now to prevent issues.

- *Enhanced physical development.* It is much easier to walk, run, and play without a diaper on.

- *Decreased risk of infectious diarrhea and Hepatitis A.* When your child sits in his feces, he is more likely to become infected by those little microscopic critters that like to hang out in feces.

- *Decreased occurrence of diaper rash.* The most effective way to clear up diaper rash is to stop using diapers.

- *Lifelong healthy bowel habits and a healthy lifestyle.* Listening to your body when you need to go, honoring your body's processes, and being patient while the poop goes into a place that is hygienic and socially proper...everyone deserves this level of health.

TROUBLESHOOTING:
THE SOLUTIONS & OTHER
SPECIFICS

The following is a compilation of all the solutions I've found, gathered, researched (and filtered) for the most common potty training questions. They are listed alphabetically. Should you need more assistance, you may gain lifetime access to our private peer-based support group by visiting godiaperfree.com/ptupgrade.

Note: Please do not read this section _unless_ you are _actually_ experiencing a problem. Some people do not have a potty training problem in the world...and reading this section may actually *cause* problems to manifest through the *anticipation and* (hopeful) *prevention* of them. Please only read the following solutions IF you are experiencing a challenge.

(And if you are experiencing a challenge, you are in the right place, and you are not alone.)

OVERALL

"Almost all problems can be solved by relieving any kind of pressure, whether it be pressure to maintain a social calendar, to prove yourself, to do this right, or to potty train in exactly three days or fewer" (Glowacki, 2013).

If you are hovering, hyperfocusing on pottying, or putting pressure on your child by continuously offering and asking if she needs to go, turn down your intensity a few notches and offer less.

Do not fully back off, do not re-diaper, do not regress in your teachings, and most of all, do not let your own fear of your child and/or the process get you down. Instead, simply tone it down a bit, focus on connection and other things in your parenting life, and allow for more autonomy and space in your pottying habits.

For most potty training difficulties, remind/prompt, turn your back, pretend to do something else, walk away, whatever…and offer a tiny bit less.

ACCIDENTS

Accidents, or "misses" in EC terminology, happen. They are excellent learning opportunities for both of you. *Always strive to learn from an accident, or "missed" opportunity.*

There are a lot of little sub-sections in this category.

Please read through to see which will help you most.

Handling accident clean-up. Back in the how-to part of this book I shared one of our Montessori teacher reader's methods of handling wet pants. Please go to the troubleshooting section "Montessori" to read it again.

Sudden accidents – life transitions. If you've had consistent success and are faced with sudden accidents, zoom out to see the big picture of your toddler's present-day life. Is he sick? Did she just start daycare? Did you move or start a new job? Is she getting those 2 year molars? Are you and your partner arguing a lot?

Try to figure out what's underlying the sudden accidents and *do not return to using diapers*, no matter what you do. Then, address those underlying issues in any way you can. Treat the teething pain. Help her adjust to daycare. Treat the illness. Get some couples' counseling. Fix that underlying problem as best you can, and understand that all major life transitions affect potty behavior. All of them.

Read on for what to do if there is no sudden transition and you are having sudden accidents….

Sudden accidents – wants full control. Please read the troubleshooting topic "Resistance" to learn about dealing with a lot of sudden accidents and associated resistance. It's actually a moment in potty training that is quite common…**your child is asking for more control over the process through increased accidents and resistance.** The answer lies in reducing your prompting and giving him more privacy. That section will tell you more.

If you aren't facing sudden accidents, but just those annoying ongoing ones, here are some more thoughts.

Won't leave play to potty. Sometimes our more active children are so focused on their tasks that they forget to take a break. He may just leak a little to relieve the pressure and keep on playing, resulting in a string of tiny pre-pee wets.

Or she will have full-on wet pants because she waited way too long and couldn't hold it any longer. Remember, if there is too much pressure on those sphincters, they will simply release!

How to prevent an accident during playtime? Prompt him to go intermittently based on the natural timing of his usual pees. If he fusses about not being able to keep playing, have him bring his toy with him, offer the toy the potty first, then your child, and then return him to play. Say something like, "It's time to go potty, then you can finish building that in just a second. Bring that piece with you."

After any accident, stay calm and don't get mad at her, but also **do not say, "That's okay,"** which approves the *behavior*.

You can (and, I'd say, *should*) verbally disapprove of the behavior by being honest and saying, "No, {name}, peepee goes in the potty, not in your pants. Let's go change and see if you have any more peepee in there to put in the potty."

Why sugarcoat it? You're not condemning her, but you certainly do not *actually* want pee in the pants, nor on the floor, so be honest with her. **It is AOK to honestly set a boundary for your child.**

Have her help you clean up any mess on the floor and help change her own clothing. Do all of this in the bathroom, encouraging her to do as much of the process of changing as possible (as in the Montessori example).

At this time, offer the potty anyway, as you would have had he *not* had an accident. Give him a chance to finish in the potty. Oftentimes he's got more where that came from, as the act of starting to wet his pants had only startled him into pausing mid-pee.

Pre-pees and little tinkles. Sometimes children will "pre-pee" in their undies in order to let off some of the pressure so they can play just a little bit longer. Discourage this by noticing peepee dances, bringing awareness to your child when you see a dance

105

but she doesn't (*I see you dancing around and grabbing your crotch…let's go potty real quick and then get you back to playing*), and also relying on the transition times and natural timing that you learned when you did Phase 1, Step 1, of the potty training experience.

Experimentation. At other times, your child may test the limits of how long he can hold it. This may end in an accident, as when that sphincter can not hold any longer, it just opens right up. In the spirit of learning, remind him how to get to the bathroom when he feels peepee in his belly (or when he does his peepee dance). Also, offer just to make sure there isn't any more pee inside her.

Staying calm. Keep in mind that kids don't *want* to have accidents, and they can range from not caring about them to feeling very ashamed. Know your unique child and stay calm.

Remind your child, "Next time let's get that pee in the potty," and put some dry pants on together.

Overall, be *matter-of-fact* in the face of an accident. Be *honest*. And do not emotionally react or become punitive. If you react in a negative manner (other than plainly disapproving of the behavior), your child may do it again just to get a rise out of you.

They sure do know our hot buttons, these kiddos!

Don't worry if you *do* get mad…it will not permanently ruin potty training or your relationship with your child. It will not psychologically damage your child. Teach her self- forgiveness by modeling it. Apologize for yelling. And next time, be more plain and even if an accident occurs.

To reiterate, be matter-of-fact and give less attention for an accident, honestly show you don't approve of it without punishing him, clean up quickly and together with him, and give positive attention when pee *does* go in the potty.

Be prepared. Be prepared…on outings and at home…with a change of clothes, the proper cleaning supplies, and the right attitude: the attitude of a teacher whose student is overall doing great and just needs a little more help til she can completely do it herself.

If you are out running errands and do not have enough changes of clothing with you, it will probably result in you stressing and your child feeling anxiety and shame. Be prepared!

And no need to feel embarrassed about a public accident…if there is a parent watching he or she will absolutely have been there before. We've all been there.

BEDTIME, STALLED

If you *expect* several false cries for "I need to pee," which can effectively stall bedtime, and instead *integrate* the time needed for them by moving bedtime prep up by 45 minutes, you may eradicate them over time.

Alternatively, give your child a set number of pre-bed potty attempts, and then say no. Perhaps you give her three opportunities, and if she continues to cry wolf, any request thereafter will be denied. *You can have one more try and then you will need to hold it til morning.*

At our house, we do "final peepee" and "final drink of water" and that is it. No further requests are ever honored. We simply say, "You already went. Now go to sleep." The kids magically stop asking!

Here's an exception: Some children genuinely don't have to go while walking around before bedtime, but the moment they lay down, they really need to pee. The sudden relaxation inspires a potty trip. Honor this request at 5-10 minutes after they are put down for bed, but make it very matter-of-fact and businesslike. No chitchat, no playing, and right back to bed.

BEDWETTING

We are going to look at genuine bedwetting problems and the issue of regular nighttime accidents separately.

Bedwetting is becoming more and more common, and I have some assumptions as to why it's gotten so widespread. If a child is put in a PullUp or other disposable diaper at night, there is *no reason* for him to hold his pee, and he will continue to wet at night for several more years. There is nothing learned, nothing gained, by having this night diaper on for 4, 5, or 6 years. A child has to learn some day. So, many "bedwetters" are not actually *medically* wetting…they are wetting because there has never been any teaching to do otherwise. Parents are afraid to take the plunge and night train.

On the other hand, some bedwetters do so regardless of what they wear to bed. The root of bedwetting is either physiological (will pass in time as the body develops) or hereditary (one or both of the parents were bedwetters as children). Either way, this a medical, not behavioral, issue. If your child wets the bed beyond 6 years old, speak to your pediatrician. Experts can offer you bladder-training exercises, therapy, medication, and diet change recommendations when regular night toilet training does not do the job. These same experts say that before 6 years of age it is difficult to tell whether the bedwetting is medical or will pass...so at 6 years you can be pretty certain of a diagnosis.

If your child is not really a bedwetter (or you aren't sure yet), but **you are having nighttime accidents quite regularly**, you may need to wake your child at 10pm and 2am, or whenever his nighttime pee intervals are (see the Nighttime training section of this book), or when you go to bed yourself or wake to pee, and/or you may need to monitor his nighttime fluids (2 hours before bed) much more strictly.

You may also wish to try a nighttime potty alarm (talk to your pediatrician or pharmacist for more information).

If your child **suddenly begins wetting at night after many months of dry nights**, you may want to see your pediatrician and rule out possible underlying issues, such as urinary tract infections or other illness. I also encourage you to zoom out in your own life and see if there is a major transition going on, or note if a developmental step is being reached within your child. These things can cause sudden accidents to happen at night, and you can clear them up by easing any anxiety or illness directly.

What to do when a child wets the bed...if it's not too disturbing to her sleep or her mood, have her try to finish on the potty to make sure her bladder is empty before you put her in dry pajamas. Remove the top layer of sheets and mattress protection if you've double-made the bed, or place a thick fleece blanket on top of the peed-on sheets and have your child sleep on top of this, changing the soiled sheets in the morning. It will not leak through. Or, invite your child into the bed with you if you are open to it, and change the sheets in the morning.

Overall, bedwetting is currently somewhat common in children under 6 years of age. It never requires punishment, and with older children they can help you clean up and get themselves back to bed. Teach your child to remain calm and take care of them in stride.

Do not use diapers at night once you've night-trained, use extra protection if your child has night accidents, and be patient...this won't last forever.

As a final tip for an occasional night wetter...one thing we did with my son is have him sleep naked inside of footed, fleece pajamas. One accident in those and he never peed the bed again, unless he was sick.

You know your child best and can use that knowledge and a little bit of creativity to work with her at night.

BEHAVIOR

With any problem in potty training, you can differentiate whether it's a potty training problem or a behavioral problem by setting boundaries and sticking to them. So long as you stand firm in your overall family boundaries (and make some if you don't have them already), behavioral issues will be corrected and actual potty training problems can be more easily isolated. They will bubble to the top.

A quick aside: If you aren't the boundary-setting type, please go and read *Mean Moms Rule*, *Simplicity Parenting*, and/or *Bringing up Bébé*. All three of these books are wonderful at teaching how to provide clear boundaries for your children so that, within them, they can feel safe and free to choose from all of the possibilities *within* that boundary. Without clear boundaries, our children become overly "spirited" or "strong-willed." Some kids are born spirited or strong-willed, but most of them are *made into* those descriptions.

Bottom line: our children become extremely anxious (and act out) when we are child-led or child-centered. They don't want to be in charge. They *do* want to choose whether to wear the red shirt or the blue shirt, but they do *not* want to schedule their own days and choose their bedtimes...and choose whether to stop using diapers or not. (*The Continuum Concept* goes into great detail about this and is a wonderful read.)

The topic of boundaries extends beyond the scope of this book, so I offer the three titles above if you need some support in this area of boundary-setting, or if you are curious. They are the real deal. No spanking, no authoritarianism, total respect for our children, *and* they teach us how to be the type of parents we wish we could be.

So, back to potty training. Any behavior you would frown upon in your non-potty-training days must be equally frowned upon *during* potty training. She will test you. Stand firm in what your family's expected boundaries and rules are.

Example: It's time for dinner. Do you allow your child to run around and feed him in spurts *as* he runs laps in the living room? Or do you *require* him to sit down at the dinner table with the rest of the family and eat his meal there?

Would you like your later teenage child to eat with her family, or to grab a snack and eat in front of the TV in her bedroom? What is your long-term boundary there?

If you can set a boundary and tell your child to sit down for dinner, you can tell your child to sit down to pee.

If you have trouble sitting your child down for dinner, and you *wish* you *didn't* have trouble doing so, because it feels *right* to have him sit for it, read those three books above, because you may also find that you have trouble sitting your child down for a pee.

If you don't believe children should sit for dinner, that's your choice, and I encourage you to consider how you are preparing her for the rest of her life. Will she be equipped to follow traffic laws and boss' requests? Will she succeed in school? Are you setting her up for lifetime success (which involves good internal and external boundaries)?

If you aren't, and this hits a vein with you, read those three books sooner than later. If you are lax on boundaries because your parents were too strict with you as a child, find a middle ground. The extremes aren't healthy (no boundaries vs. too strict). In the end I realize it's your personal choice...*and* it will help with difficulties in potty training to have a good sense of parental boundaries.

So, in potty training we are not *forcing* our children to do anything. We want to remain really positive and neutral, yes? Good. And boundaries are important to this process.

If you say something firmly, you are still being gentle. You've had to firmly strap an unwilling child into the carseat, yes? Same thing here. The pee and poo *have* to go in the potty now that there are no diapers.

Be firm and unwavering without being forceful or negative. Firm is clear, and clear is gentle.

If your child was doing great for a few days and now outright refuses or claims he can longer use the potty, it is behavioral. He's pottied successfully more than once by this point. That means he *can*. He is *capable*. He has *demonstrated* success.

What to do? Set a boundary with an immediate consequence and follow through on it. *If you will not leave your play for the potty, I will take away this toy until you do.* Then follow through with it.

Example: He refuses to leave his train table to go pee, despite doing an obvious peepee dance. You take the toy he's playing with away and say, "I will give you Gordon back *after* you go put your pee in the potty." If he goes and pees at that time, you give Gordon back (and you confirm that this was <u>behavioral</u>, not a potty training issue!).

If he doesn't do it, despite the consequence, then you simply need to teach more. It is a <u>potty training </u>issue. Do more teaching days. Work on some weaker areas with him. Teach all the little things to ensure there are no gaps in knowledge. Usually a gap in knowledge (unknown to you) causes apathy towards pottying. Your child doesn't give a damn because he actually needs more teaching and more information. See "Doesn't Care."

I advocate clear and immediate consequences for behavior that breaks (or upholds) our "family rules," which my children helped come up with at a family meeting. These consequences are all related to the offense, they are quickly and gently administered, and they are always followed through on. They aren't used to threaten my kids, they are used to reinforce positive behavior (yes, I give positive consequences like a pat on the back or a hug or a "good job") and to discourage negative behavior (hitting someone will land you a 5 minute time out).

(By the way, a time-out doesn't work for potty training…from child's the point of view it is not relevant to the offense.)

If you have family rules (or need to write some down!), you've listed out the expectations of every member of your family. They might resemble the following: We *do not* hit.

We *do* give gentle hugs. We *do not* talk nasty to one another. We *do* speak kindly. We *do not* wet our pants. We *do* put our pee in the potty.

Lastly, if you have a child who is using pee or poop as a "weapon" against you, I first offer compassion and empathy, and second, I recommend that you find a professional to do play therapy with him or her.

Using pee or poop as a weapon (example: she didn't get her way so she stares directly at you and pees on the floor with a spiteful look on her face) is a symptom of deep- seated anger or emotional difficulty. Work that out with a professional.

BOYS

First of all, it's not true that boys always take longer than girls to potty train. Boys are much more physical, usually, and are just different from girls, that's all.

It's a good idea to teach boys to sit on the potty for *both* pee and poo at first, as the sensation to go will feel like one in the same. When you are ready to teach him how to pee standing up, have another male family member or friend teach him how, outdoors or in the bathroom. Use a stool if that helps. They also make tiny urinals, found at godiaperfree.com/urinal. It's okay to put this off for several years until your boy expresses a desire to "do it like dad," or until your son gets taller.

When you teach him how to pee standing up, please also teach him how to raise and lower the lid. If he makes a mess, have him clean it up. If you want to do target practice, be my guest! Throw some O's in there or pieces of toilet paper and have him spray them with his firehose.

If you have the issue of pee shooting over the front of the potty or toilet when he is sitting to pee, you are not alone. It doesn't matter whether your son is circumcised or not, pee can go everywhere. A good solution is to have your son scoot back a little on the potty and lean slightly forward. Another solution is to get a toilet seat reducer with a tall rubber pee guard (the ones I recommend in the Supply List, made by Ginsey, are great for this).

Or use a bathroom mat or towel underneath the potty until things get a little more under control.

You can also teach your son how to aim his penis by guiding his hand to it and helping him aim it downward.

If your son plays with his penis while naked (or reaches into his undies to do so), you can teach him to be socially appropriate and not do such things in public, or only allow him to do that in the bathtub or while at home.

The biological and instinctual purpose for tugging at his penis at such a young age is to stretch and condition the foreskin (it is deeply instinctual, whether your son has a foreskin or not). Now, when he becomes a teenager, we have a different set of reasons for all that tugging! But for now, it's totally normal and innocent for him to play with his parts.

Teach your son to wash his hands after handling his penis and to use courtesy with any mess he makes by cleaning it up.

Lastly, a bit of trivia: most boys get a partial erection prior to urinating, especially as wee babies. I imagine that physiologically this helps the pee shoot far from the body, and keeps the child clean. So, if your boy is naked and you notice what we call a "peenie weenie" (in EC lingo), it may be a signal that he needs to pee.

CONSTIPATION

Symptoms of problematic constipation include if your child "has not passed a stool and is acting uncomfortable, not eating, having fever, vomiting, or looking listless or ill in any way" (Lekovic, 2006). If you notice any of these symptoms, call your pediatrician right away. Encopresis is something that should be addressed immediately.

If your child is eating well, turns red and grunts during pooping, passes normal-looking stool, and seems to be healthy in all other ways, then he is not medically constipated.

If your baby passes pebble-like stools that are hard and round, then you may be dealing with simple constipation where a small, temporary dietary change may make the poop a little softer and easier to pass.

It is pretty normal for a child to withhold his poop for a day or two at the start of potty training. If it's clear to you that he's having pain, and has simple constipation, you can help things along with dietary changes. If this has been a constant issue for you, check in with a professional to see if there is a food allergy you're missing, or permanently change her diet. Or try some of the below.

The first, most benign thing you can try is giving a pouch or two of pureed prunes. Plum Organics makes an excellent line of pouch foods for babies and toddlers, and if your child is constipated one or two pouches of their Just Prunes product will do the trick (found at your local grocery store or online at godiaperfree.com/justprunes). If your child isn't constipated, the prunes won't hurt or give him the runs. Prunes are pretty great.

A teaspoon or two of coconut milk or coconut oil is helpful, as over-use of fibers can constipate further, and oils do the opposite. Makes sense, doesn't it? Oils move things along quite nicely.

Make sure your child is hydrating throughout the day with plenty of water and some juice if you're into that. Limit constipating foods for a few days, such as bananas, white rice, cheese, applesauce, soda, and orange juice. Increase foods that do not constipate, such as whole grains, veggies, and fruits.

You may want to put some petroleum jelly or other more natural balm like this one by Earth Mama Angel Baby - godiaperfree.com/balm - around his rectum before he has a movement, or just in general. Make sure he's getting enough exercise, too.

See if you can get a potty that inspires a deeper squat. Historically, humans have eliminated while squatting. Our modern toilets do not help us get into this optimum position.

The bEcoPotty is good for this. You can also put a stool below your big toilet, or the taller adult Squatty Potty (godiaperfree.com/squattypotty), to help your child with that squat position.

If diet or these other ideas don't solve simple constipation, look at the whole situation, and especially your part in it. Do you have a poop aversion? Constipation problems yourself? Are you so freaked that he hasn't pooped in the potty for 2 days (or perhaps forecasting that he will be afraid of pooping in the potty because of stories you've read) that you are stressing him the heck out? Again, not pooping the first 2 days of potty training is normal. Let's not make it worse by freaking out.

If you are, work on that inside yourself and come back to the matter at hand. Relax about poop. Everybody poops. Poop in front of your child and show her how it's done.

Work on getting over your poop issues and your child will follow suit (if it's not just dietary, or medical).

And, by the way, you aren't alone. Poop complexes are a regular thing in today's Western society. It's normal (for now). We are a rushed, overscheduled society. You can't rush poop.

CRYING

Some children cry when faced with *anything* new, changed, or different. You know if you have a child like this. This is sort of her blanket response to change.

If your child cries during potty training, reassure her while staying clear and brief in your teachings. He most likely cried when he had to be strapped into the carseat for the first time, or the high chair, or had to take a nap when he didn't want to. This is no different.

Please don't try to solve all of your child's cries by giving her what she wants, on-demand. I call this hyper-responsiveness, which we all naturally practiced with our newborns (as it was 100% needed). When we continue to be hyper-responsive with our toddlers, it can become quite detrimental. When she's older, you will have quite a whiner on your hands (or maybe you already do!).

Instead, endure the cries, make the environment consistent and your direction steadfast, and she will see that you mean business, you're in charge, and she'll feel safe (whether she drops the crying bit or not, but it's likely that she will).

See also "Resistance" and "Tantrums."

DAYCARE AND CAREGIVERS

First, to quell any fear you may have, lack of cooperation from your daycare will not derail potty training. It is not make-or-break. Potty train anyway. Eventually your daycare will catch on, mostly through your and your child's insistence and follow-through. Stick with it. And be open to the surprise that your daycare may be open to having a potty-trained child in their classroom! It does happen.

An open and honest conversation (privately, not in the presence of your child, if possible) is the first clear step in enlisting your daycare to support your potty training. A partnership is what you seek. Find out their policies, their normal toileting routine, and let them know, with confidence and clarity, that you are potty training, will be complete with it soon, and would like their support with what you are doing.

Oftentimes daycares have loads of experience with supporting toilet training. Even though the ages are getting higher and higher with potty independence, and PullUps policies are the norm for ages 1-3, most daycares have been in business for a good many years. Not too long ago, their policies were different. Find out their current routines and see if there is anything you two need to negotiate to best support your unique child in staying clean and dry at daycare.

Request that you may bring your child in with cloth training pants or underwear with a waterproof cover at first, transitioning eventually away from the cover. If they need a toilet seat reducer, give them one so they have the tools they need to support your work.

Pick one teacher and show her your child's signals or peepee dance and inform her of your child's natural timing (how often she pees: every 45 minutes, hour, hour and a half, whatever it is). Demonstrate how you do not ask but *state* that it is potty time. Show her how you get your child onto the potty, and her overall routine. Describe and demonstrate. Tell her where you're at with clothing manipulation and what you're working on right now.

With an in-home caregiver, she also may have her pre-formed opinions about how potty training should or should not go. Tell her you're potty training, ask for her experience with it, opinions on it, and show her how you do what you've done in potty training your young one (or what your plan is so she'll be on-board). Do all of what I described in the last paragraph and tell him or her that, over time, s/he (the caregiver) will get the hang of it. Typically, when a caregiver thinks that the child needs a diaper change, they are actually picking up on the fact that the child is signaling that she needs to go pee. You can ask your caregiver to listen to this form of potty intuition and act upon it.

Some caregivers who come from other countries will be happy to support you in maintaining diaper-free status, as many come from cultures where diapers are not common.

Your caregiver might even have a magic touch with potty-related things. Find out what she knows or how they did things in her country of origin.

The bottom line about daycares and caregivers: you're the boss. You pay them, and you should not have to compromise your potty training efforts or timeline because they don't want to help in this process. It's a conversation that needs to take place. If your child isn't having poop accidents, generally your daycare will agree to whatever you're doing (if you're certain about it).

In many preschool and all kindergarten situations, there are rules that children *must* be potty trained…which is obviously in your benefit. Why not start now?

When you think about it, this developmental task should be focused on above and beyond the pre- development of reading and writing skills in your 2 or 3 year old. Potty training is an important emotional and physical step that should receive attention by caregivers. Getting a head start on academics comes second, in my opinion and experience.

If daycare is not on board…potty train anyway and come back "done." Then they pretty much won't have a choice, will they?

Here's how. Take some extra days off both work and daycare to focus on completing your toilet training endeavor at home. Learn your child's exact pee routine post-waking and post-drinking, and get it down pat. Write it down if you need to. Teach your child by prompting him with what you want him to say to you (or anyone) when he needs to pee.

The goal is to come back to daycare from your several days' break with a precise knowledge of your child's natural timing and peepee dance/signals, with your child already asking to go to the bathroom, and without a diaper on her (a naptime diaper at daycare is an exception, for now, if they require it).

Orient your child to the daycare's bathroom and toilet.

Donate that seat if they don't have one. If there isn't a bathroom nearby, ask if you can put a mini potty in the room. Familiarity with the bathroom is *essential* for your child to feel supported in expressing his need to go.

Next, tell your child *Ms. Nancy will help you pee when you need to go. Tell her "potty" and she will take you.* Follow what I've written in the paragraphs above to teach *one* of the teachers the ropes of what you and your child have achieved with potty training at home, and tell your child to tell the teacher (or to signal to her with a wave or tug) every single time he needs to go. Select the teacher who is most open to and patient with this sort of thing. Do not worry about teaching the other teachers unless it's necessary (such as if one of them is only there once a week).

If you give the daycare teacher your child's natural timing (her intervals), the teacher can potty her at those times and those times only. If you know the peepee dance, share that with her as I've discussed above. Make sure the teacher pauses your child's play and saves his toy for him while he goes off to the bathroom, and make sure that she doesn't hover over him when she takes him. Tell her to be casual and give privacy in the ways that you know will work.

Be really brief with your instructions for the daycare teacher, and really clear with your child. *Take her every 40 minutes, her peepee dance is grabbing her crotch or walking to the bathroom door, and she will also tell you "potty" when she needs to go. And…honey, here is the bathroom. Ms. Nancy will take you when you need to go, just tell her "potty" like you do at home.*

They have a potty just for you, just like the one at home.

Tell your child if he's the only child in class who is potty training or which other kids are also doing it right now. He will notice! And he will feel proud.

And then continue to work things out *together* with your caregiver(s). Be *steadfast* in your decision to train *now* and get really clear with how things work and look in the day-to-day reality. Then communicate that info, briefly, with the caregivers…not as an option, but as a *requirement* of what your child is doing now.

If you're not having success at home, don't be embarrassed or feel like a failure. Ask the daycare if they can try with your child when he's there. Some kids do great when the parents aren't around, and this could really help your situation if potty training is slow-going at home. It's not an admittance of defeat to say you're not having success at home. Just say, *Hey, I could really use your help with this.*

Could you please potty her every 45 minutes here and let me know what worked for you two?

Worst-case scenario…if your daycare requires diapers and there is no way around it, continue your diaper-free life at home and tell her she has to wear a diaper at daycare, for now, because that is Ms. Nancy's rule (or whomever). You can stick a piece of cut-up washcloth in the diaper so she retains her sensitivity to wetness. Potty her when you get to daycare, right as you pick her up, and if you come to visit during the hours she's there.

If the daycare insists on disposable diapers and you don't feel it's in your child's best interest, find another daycare that is cloth-friendly (and who would, in turn, be most likely to allow undies or training pants). If it's important enough to you, you will probably want to find a better match in caregivers.

One of our community members couldn't convince her daycare that her 24 month old was potty trained, so she filmed a video of her child initiating and going to the bathroom at home, showed it to the teacher, and the teacher was so impressed that she enthusiastically allowed this child to wear undies instead of a diaper, and use the potty, at daycare. You just never know….

DOESN'T CARE

If your child has the attitude that she just doesn't care about whether she's wet or dry, uses the potty or her pants, and could care less about the whole process, she is likely shutting down because she can't do it very well yet. Some bit is missing; something needs more teaching; she hasn't mastered it all, so why bother?

Which part is he struggling with? Well, there's really no telling. There is, however, a lack in knowledge that is causing him to shut down and act like he no longer cares about this thing.

You may have had the same experience in your life…you quit something because you just weren't good enough, and whether you realized it or not, if you'd had just a tiny bit more instruction and guidance, you probably would have stuck with that thing, right? And you might have been great at it, too.

So, for your child, go through Phase 1 once more, Steps 1, 2, and 3, quickly and all over again. Quickly go back through the whole process in an abbreviated manner. See if you notice what's missing, or where she struggles. Is it between naked and clothed outings? Naked at home and clothing at home? These are common places where there's a gap in information, and a little more practice will go a long way. Your child lacks confidence and will benefit from more learning.

Strengthen the skills by repeating those sections until she has them all. Be consistent, patient, and clear. Then she will begin to care because she feels *successful* at this whole pottying thing.

EC, COMPLETION

In my first book I wrote a section on completing EC for those who've done any amount of EC prior to 18 months of age. I also recommended that some parents may want to wrap up EC with a potty training experience. This new book you're reading *is* just that experience.

If you've done some EC in the past and perhaps things never clicked, things never wrapped up, or you just want to seal the deal once your child has hit 18 months, here's what to do:

Use this book's potty training plan verbatim, potty training just as you would had there never been any EC in your life.

As simple as that. The reason is that your child may be missing something that the potty training experience will absolutely teach. This book's method of potty training will help to fill in those gaps and move you both from "pee goes in the potty as much as you can, dear" to "pee goes in the potty every single time."

The frame of mind you're in when you follow this book is also different from the EC frame of mind…EC is very flexible, but with this book, you are not going to be as lenient as you would be with a younger toddler or baby. Instead, you've switched gears into preparing your very capable toddler for doing the *whole thing* himself.

If you don't follow this whole plan to finish up EC, and you skip around and only do the parts of potty training that *you* think your child needs, it may work for you, or you may miss a tiny opportunity for learning that you didn't realize was missing. It could be anything.

So, go ahead and do the whole process (with the exception of saying "we are throwing out the diapers," of course!).

Also, doing potty training to wrap up EC does *not* mean that you've failed at EC. EC has historically (for the past 40 years since it's been in the Western world) been a gradual process with no focus on completion…because *focus on completion* was thought to have derailed the non- pressured process.

However, with my work over several years and with several thousand parents, it's become clear that potty training is sometimes essential in wrapping up EC with most children. A potty training experience provides a clear finish for a process that has often dragged on because no one has ever given parents a clear *endpoint* for EC. We EC educators are all still learning, and this combination of EC and potty training is a great revelation! This is your answer.

In this book you will see me say, time and again, that toddlers have different needs than babies.

I commend you for having tended to your baby's needs with EC, whose goal was never potty *training*, and I also commend you for wrapping up EC *with* potty training.

If you're using this book to wrap up EC, you are one resourceful parent! You're awesome.

(And if you have no idea what EC is but are interested in using it with your next baby, learn about my other book at godiaperfree.com/thebook.)

FEAR, IN GENERAL

If your child is afraid of *anything* to do with the potty process, the first step is to check in with your own energy around potty training (your "vibe," if you will). Is it anxious, strained, pressured, upset, ambivalent, fearful, cautious, or perfectionistic? **Check in with your potty training vibe first.** Then, work on shifting your energy to a more neutral, matter-of-fact, *it's just what we do* vibe; a less fearful state of being; a more confident state of being.

After doing that, let's take a look at your child's general potty training fear.

Do not invalidate or dismiss his feelings, but at the same time, don't feed the fire and make it worse. "Yes, this is new to you, <u>and </u>this is what were doing now."

If you are the kind of parent who reacts to a little fall with an overabundance of moans, hugs, kisses, and exclamations like "you poor sweet baby, did that hurt sooo much?" then you may find this difficult. As in those boo-boo situations, if we remain neutral yet caring, our children calm down way faster because they've know: *if mom or dad's not worried about me, I must be okay.* (For example, I wait to see if my child is really hurt or not, and if she is I always offer a shoulder to cry on, but I don't reinforce it by commiserating…it just makes it worse.)

Your fear of her *possibly* getting afraid or upset during potty training, or your expectation of her fear, will actually create or reinforce her fear. Not long ago, she was in utero feeling everything you felt. We are not too far removed from that arrangement, and our children continue to be *very* connected to our vibe, energy level, and emotions for many more years. It's *telepathic*, to use some Ina May 60's terminology.

So, for an overall fear of potty training fix, check yourself and then put it into neutral.

FEAR OF FLUSHING

Fear of the loud public toilet flush is very common, even among younger children (and yours truly). Toilets have gotten really loud, and with a small child on the seat, the sensors often cause an autoflush before it's convenient.

Bring a pad of Post-It Notes to put over the auto sensor on public autoflush toilets.

For regular toilets, whether at home or in a store, have your child flush it himself so that he can control when the sound comes out and "feel" the power of it a little more directly. This takes some of the mystery out of it...and the fear.

Teaching flushing as part of an overall bathroom routine will also *normalize* flushing as "something we do."

You can also flush it after your child leaves the room (at home) or after she leaves the stall for a time, then slowly integrate flushing it while she's still in there with you, not as a solo "we are now flushing" experience, but casually while talking or cleaning something up. If you don't give it attention or put too much energy into persuading her into liking it, she will probably start to ignore it as you do.

Matter-of-fact...works every time.

To get your child to begin flushing, you can always put a square of toilet paper in and watch together as it disappears. Offer a little statement about where the water goes, what we do if our toilet gets stopped up (call a plumber or use the plunger), or whatever else you think your son or daughter might like to learn. Get a book on those topics from the library if you feel so inclined.

My son was fascinated when he learned about sewers.

He was never afraid of the flushing part because we practiced infant potty training with him from birth, but he, to this day, despises the autoflushers in public restrooms, and always asks, "Does this bathroom have loud toilets or quiet toilets?" prior to entering. Too cute.

FEAR OF POOPING IN POTTY

The most obvious reason for fear of pooping in the potty is that your child has never done it before. Having warm squishy poop against her skin is the norm. It is comfortable, even. It is all she has ever known.

Having the poop leave her body after years of the opposite can provoke anxiety in children. Some kids believe the poop is part of them and are freaked out by it "falling out."

Not all kids. I repeat, not all kids. But some. So please don't expect it, but if it happens to you, understand that it is not a reason to call your pediatrician.

The solution for this is to acknowledge and validate his fear without making it worse…and to confirm that this is the new norm. Commiserating is not appropriate here.

Say something like, *I know this is a strange feeling, and this is where your poopoo goes now.*

Deal with the fear as you would deal with any other fear your child tells you about.

The monsters are in my closet and I can't go to sleep! How do you handle that one? Handle the fear of pooping in the potty in the same, exact way.

Be stern and creative at the same time. Perhaps a toy can be his potty guard, or can poop in the potty first to show that it's okay for him to go next.

Poop in your toilet while your child's on her potty in the bathroom with you. (Yes, you!) Show her that it's no big deal. Poop together. *I'm in this with you, dear.* Literally.

If your child is obsessed with your iPhone or iPad, whip that sucker out, just to get past this bit. No shame in that, for the first few times. After a little while though, don't offer devices at potty time. Potty time is strictly business. We go, we clean up, we're done.

Also, you may want to try the **toss-it-out prompt**. Say, "It's time to poop," be sure he's got all his equipment at hand and/or out of the way (pants down), and then leave the room, pretending to have forgotten something. I always do a countdown to ease that *she left the room* anxiety…5, 4, 3, 2, 2 ½, 2 ¾, 1. And when you return, it's likely that he's pooped in his potty.

If you fear escape, close the door. If your child would freak out if you left and closed the door, stay in the bathroom, busy yourself with something else, and ignore her while the door is closed (with both of you in there). If you see a poop begin out of the corner of your eye (because you are actually paying attention, ninja-style), and your child is not on the potty, transport during that poop calmly and coolly.

For more info on prompting, please see that section in Phase 2.

FEAR OF TOILET/POTTY

Fear is not the same thing as resistance. **Somewhat fearful** is pretty common, whereas extremely fearful is extremely rare.

Again, we are going to validate her feelings *and* add some common sense into the mix.

Yes, I know it feels weird to you, and this is where you pee or…

This is new for you, huh? Let's check it out and see what this potty is all about.

And help him explore it. *See, it's made of plastic. Pick it up. Is it light or heavy? Let's put some water in it and practice dumping the water into the big toilet.*

You could even sit on it, yourself, to demonstrate how un-scary it is. I've peed in one before when my son was 13 months and I was doing EC with him. That was the only way I could teach him how to mount the potty without another child around to demonstrate.

Speaking of, if you have another child in your neighborhood who is potty trained, invite him or her over to demonstrate. Seeing another child sit on the potty can move mountains for your child. You can also find a video on YouTube of a child sitting on a potty.

If it's a seat reducer she's afraid of or not taking to, your child might do better with a mini potty. If that doesn't do the trick, perhaps a step stool in front of the big toilet/seat reducer will make her feel more stable. I always recommend seat reducers with handles so the child can feel very secure.

And padded with some awesome characters on it (whether you actually watch TV or not) always helps with comfort, and company. See the Supply List in this book.

And do not ask, "Oh, are you afraid of your potty?!" and make it into a big deal for him. He will say "yes" whether he is or not. He will feed off of that woeful attention and pull you into believing that the sky is, indeed, falling.

You lead the way by not bringing fear words into it and not feeding the fire.

During Phase 1, you will have plenty of practice bringing your child to the potty mid-pee. Be sure to do this part with a calm vibe and no emotion. Any fear you have will probably translate over to your child.

And a side note: if transporting him to the potty creates fear, you can always move the potty *to him* during Phase 1.

Now for the excessively fearful child (very, very rare).

If your child is completely terrified *from the very first step of potty training*, it might be genuine fear as opposed to minor fear or resistance.

What to do? With an extremely fearful child, you just have to take things a little more *slowly*.

If your child is genuinely terrified of the toilet, the feeling, or any part of this, and what I've suggested so far hasn't helped a bit, then you have probably dealt with his intense fear in other non-potty-training situations before. Use the same things that you know work with his particular temperament, and his particular flavor of fear.

With the very, very fearful child, *ask* her if she'd like to sit on the potty. Ask for her *permission*. I know, this is contrary to all I've said so far, and all I teach in my EC book as well. But the thing is, if you don't get her on board, by her own will and choice, the fear will continue to overwhelm her. Keep at it though. It may take 2 months instead of 7 days…which is fine.

If going slowly doesn't work for the very fearful child, check in and see if there is another underlying issue, physically, emotionally, or psychologically. It could be anxiety stemming from elsewhere in his life, and it would behoove you to find out.

HAS IT, THEN DOESN'T, THEN HAS IT AGAIN

If you are having the issue of a child who gets it, then doesn't, then gets it again, you may benefit from looking at yourself and **your level of commitment and consistency** with the actual toilet training (Phase 1) and the follow- through required to complete the potty independence process (Phase 2).

If you are in any way wishy-washy about potty training or the follow-up for completion, your child will *also* be wishy-washy about it. If you are doing potty training "casually" your child will respond *casually*. You'll validate your choice to take it casually by noting that she isn't really getting it anyway…when really she isn't getting it *because* you are taking it casually. Get real about it. Get serious. Stop being so casual already.

If you find that you are kind of half-assing it (and can admit it to yourself), you can make the choice to get yourself back on track. We all get tired and half-ass things as new parents!!! I know I do. But if you're having this particular problem in potty training, you could do well to give this one your full gusto. It is probably the MOST important thing.

Next possibility is that "…unexplained backsliding is usually a behavioral issue, either the result of resistance or 'laziness'" (Glowacki, 2013).

Once your child "gets it," the only reason she'll "lose it" is **behavior**. It does not mean that she doesn't get it. It means that she is resisting the process or being lazy about it.

The solution? Setting clear boundaries and immediate consequences for undesirable behaviors. Remember: Be clear.

For the first solution I just mentioned, setting clear boundaries, here is the brief version:

If your child was doing great for a few days and now outright refuses or acts like he can longer use the potty, it is behavioral. He's used the potty, willingly, more than once. He *can* do it. He is *capable*. He has *demonstrated* success.

To lose it all of a sudden is purely behavioral. To address this: Set a boundary (and a related,

immediate consequence) and follow through with it. *If you will not leave your play for the potty, I will take away your toy until you do.* Then follow through with it.

An example: He refuses to leave his train table to go pee, despite doing an obvious peepee dance. You take the toy he's playing with away and say, "I will give you Gordon back after you go put your pee in the potty. Do you want Gordon back? *[replies yes]* Okay, go pee first and then you can have him." If he goes and pees at that time, you give Gordon back (and you confirm that this was behavioral!).

If he can't do it despite the consequence, then you simply need to teach more. There is a gap in learning that needs to be filled. Have more teaching days. Work on some weaker areas with him.

Do not use time-outs for behavioral consequences in potty training. They are not relevant.

As an aside, you may benefit from giving him some more privacy and control over the process, as explained in the troubleshooting section called "Accidents," specifically in the part about having accidents all of a sudden.

INTERRUPTING PLAY

Should you interrupt play for potty time? Absolutely, yes.

There are some pretty strong parenting philosophies out there right now which advocate *never* interrupting a

child at play. However, we adults pause our "play" (work, gardening, creative endeavors, road trip driving) to pee, do we not? We must teach our children to do the same.

A friend of mine has an 18 month boy who is learning about the toilet. (She admits she is taking potty learning "casually.") She says that she absolutely, without doubt, knows when he is pooping in his diaper because he gets really quiet and plays independently at his toy table. She says she doesn't interrupt him because she wants to encourage independent play. She is so thrilled that he is playing on his own that she refuses to interrupt him, despite knowing he is pooping his diaper.

I admire and support encouraging independent play, but in this situation, his need and signal to poop trumps *her* need for him to play independently. I advised her to interrupt his play for poop time then return him to what he was working on thereafter. When we really looked at what was happening, out loud, she felt a sense of shame and realized that she did not want him soiling himself…it felt inhumane to her upon admitting it. So, she is now working on interrupting him to poop when this happens.

The first solution here is to not *ask* your child if she needs to pee during playtime. You will mostly get a "no" with this approach. Instead, it must be a statement. *I see you're grabbing your peenie…time to pee. Bring tractor with you.*

If your child resists pausing her playtime for potty time (pee or poo), bring the toy with you both and encourage her to offer the potty to her toy first. Or you can potty her toy briefly and then put her on the potty next, or tell her it's her turn so she can sit, herself. The more "do it yourself," the better.

Let's put your pee in the potty so you can get back to playing.

or...

Do you want to play? Okay, let's go pee first.

If it helps your child to have a potty-time-only toy in the beginning, great! But most of the time thereafter, potty toys often distract from the task at hand. Bring the toy he was active with *only* if you're expecting a tantrum or meltdown because he has to leave playtime to potty. Have a potty-only toy *only* in the beginning stages, if it helps.

Another technique is to give a consequence if she refuses to leave playtime to potty. *It's time for you to go to the potty.* Refusal. *I will have to take your Duplos away if you do not go potty now.* She goes. Done. If she doesn't go and pees her pants instead, take the Duplos away for a short, set amount of time (follow through, by all means!) and have her clean up per the "Accidents" section.

All in all, be very matter-of-fact. *I see you squeezing your legs together. It's time to pee. Bring the doll with you.* Do the deed, then return to play.

LENGTH OF TIME TO FINISH

Children who begin potty training earlier finish with potty training earlier, every time. See *Diaper Free Before 3* if you want all the research articles, bibliography, and hard facts on this. If you trust me, just know that it's true.

Start wherever you are, today. **The sooner you start, the sooner you're finished.**

Remember that the potty training completion age has doubled since the advent of the disposable diaper in 1959. Parents before that time trained their children quickly, by 18 months of age, without coercion, rewards, force, or negative tactics. They expected the best, taught all the pieces, were consistent over several days, and supported their children's success.

You can too.

Now, when we speak of *very* young children, it may take a little longer to do the potty training process because of brain development, but there are other benefits. For instance, if you start at 16 months, it will take longer to complete vs. starting at 20 months, however, your child will experience the pride of early mastery, something she longs for regarding everything in her environment. The extra few months are indeed a gift you give to her when you train earlier. (She also gets an early taste of dignity!)

If you are interested in doing this in less time, then begin today. *That is the only way it's going to happen faster…if you put your excuses aside and just begin. And fully commit.* And completion will be earlier (and easier) the sooner you start.

MULTIPLES

Potty train your twins or triplets (or 3 year old and 2 year old, who are nearly Irish twins) **together**.

Some books will have you do it separately. I don't agree. One will see the other and the social power of "others" will kick in during this process. Train your multiples together.

Double up your team, folks! Have each person on the team read this book by sharing it directly with him or her (please limit your direct sharing to just your team…thanks!).

Set your Potty Training Experience dates at a time when your partner or mother or best friend can come help you (and stay the weekend if they don't live with you).

Have at least one person helping with training, actively training *with* you, and another person doing the household work, such as cooking, cleaning, making coffee, and pouring wine at the end of each day.

Each of you will focus on just one of the children at all times, never letting your attention off of the child while acting like you're not on them like glue (remember, ninja hovering). If you want to swap kids in the middle of the day, that is fine, just be clear as to who has whom at all times.

In the bathroom, or in the living room depending on where you choose to put the potties at first, set up TWO potty stations with TWO sets of everything needed. Also, put a small basket of

2 potty-only toys next to the potties so that when one is peeing, the other can be sitting on her potty as well or can be playing right next to the other one.

When you guys are in the bathroom, shut the door. If it's a tight fit you may not want to, but trust me: having a shut door can help reduce the chance of an escapee, and with two, you'll appreciate this.

Do not fear ditching the diapers with two kids at once.

Remember that the easiest way to potty train is by getting rid of the diapers (with both of them) once and for all.

Continue forth with potty training the both of them in the manner laid out in this book, relying on the help that you have gathered for this very special event.

And, always, follow up with a thank you gift, card, or dinner to show your appreciation to your team!

NO INTEREST

If your child lost interest in the carseat, would you stop putting her in it? If your child showed no interest in brushing his teeth, would you just never brush his teeth for a few months until he is "ready" again?

Hopefully, no and no.

Same with potty training. Yes, we aim to be gentle, but remember, we are not subscribing to the "wait for readiness" phenomenon that has been funded by the big diaper companies for 60 years.

No interest does <u>not </u>mean *put it off, give up,* or *go back to diapering til a later time when your child becomes interested again.*

Beware. *No interest* can quickly become an easy out.

Wait for readiness supports us saying "oh, she isn't showing interest, so she's just not ready. I'll try again in a few months." (And keep buying diapers.)

No. No. No.

No interest <u>actually </u>means that you, the parent, need to make potty training a priority and a non-negotiable.

If there is no medical issue, such as constipation, special needs, or UTI, then please read on.

The first thing you need to do is get serious about potty training. Read this book cover to cover, commit to it fully, and do exactly as it says.

Check in with yourself, too. Do you have serious doubts or fears around potty training? If you do, you're not alone! It is cultural and it is pervasive. Simply acknowledge those fears and get a jolt of confidence from this book. You can do it. So can your child.

Potty training should not begin when a child shows interest, and it shouldn't be given up on when a child loses interest.

All children lose interest in ALL THINGS, over time, depending on goodness-knows-what in any given moment.

Losing interest is normal!

However, **you must continue to insist** *this is what we do* **regarding the few non-negotiables that they do not have the option of losing interest in**: pottying in the correct place, eating at the dinner table, brushing teeth every day, sleeping at bedtime every night, being buckled into the carseat every single time, bathing, etc.

What are *your* non-negotiables? Take a moment, pen and paper, and make a quick list.

Add "pottying in the appropriate place" to your list and the *no interest* will become a *non-issue*.

Lastly, **do not go back to diapers** if your child loses interest. Stay the course. Who cares if she isn't "interested?" Most people drag out potty training for months or even *years* because a child loses interest. It consistently happens (especially to the most gentle of parents!). It does not mean she isn't ready. It means she's not convinced that this is the new norm.

Do not give up. Stay the course. And now might be a good time to **ditch diapers at night, too**. No diapers will make your child's "interest" irrelevant. The potty will become the *only* option, interested or not.

We parents put them into diapers in the beginning, and we parents must choose when it's time to take them out.

Therefore, their level of interest in this task is essentially irrelevant. I hope all of that makes sense. My apologies for hammering away at this one, but it is one of the most important things I can share with you.

NOT CLICKING

(See also "Doesn't care.")

"Not clicking" looks like this: your child pees her pants and clearly doesn't make any connection, have any reaction, or register anything at all.

If you're at the beginning of potty training (or in the middle) and things are not clicking, **the solution is to do another focused naked day**.

Look for *any* type of awareness during this extra day of naked teaching and observation. Does she look disgusted?

Interested? Apologetic? Thrilled? Mildly bothered? Is she hiding it from you? Does she grab her crotch? Any of those things count as awareness. And they *do* mean it's clicking. Sweet!

As a reminder, the timeline goes a little something like this: She moves from no clue –> oops, I peed –> I am peeing right now –> I need to pee. Any progression along this timeline *is* progress and means things are clicking.

So, back to the solution. During the extra focused naked day, move him to the potty at every pee and poo (or move the potty to him). "Pee goes in potty." Every time. And look for any sign of clickage (those I've listed above...they all count).

Don't hover. Remember...ninja parent style! Be *on her* but pretend like you're not that focused on her. No distractions. Learn her patterns and dances.

See if there is *any* type of "Oh, I've peed!" or "My, I'm peeing!" registering across his face. *Any* type of hiding it from you, upset that they're wet or soiled, feeling sorry for having done it, or not liking how it feels (yucky!).

If you see any of the above, it has "clicked" and you may move on to the next step in potty training (Phase 1, Step 2 and/or Step 3).

OTHER PEOPLE'S OPINIONS

Everybody's got one.

If people are getting onto you for potty training before 3 years old, or if they detect some doubt in you and challenge you about it, tune them out.

This is *your* child. YOU make the decision of when your child potty trains, not them. You know, deep down inside, that your child is capable, and you are now equipped with the knowledge to do this thing. That's enough. Everyone else can go mind his or her own business.

An immediate cure-all for the onslaught of unwelcome opinions is to stop posting your potty training status on Facebook, first and foremost. You're just opening yourself up for trouble and lots of criticism (and advice). **Just post ONCE, when you're done.** (Then recommend my book when they ask you how you did it.)

Which brings me to address unsolicited advice. If someone gives you some, simply say, *Thanks for your input! I'll consider it.* And leave it at that.

If someone insists (ahem, MILs), tell her you really appreciate her offer of help, and that you've got a plan in place already. Or say, *We're doing it already and it's working for us.* And politely change the subject.

People, whether negative critics or positive advice- givers, *want* to help. They really do. Some just go about it in extremely judgmental, unhelpful ways. Forgive them and it won't bother you as much.

Try not to be prickly in the face of others' advice. As a society, we parents have become very defensive about potty training. In fact, even as a potty training educator, I rarely tell people about my book in public. I am constantly faced with extreme defenses when broaching the subject. **So, the best thing we can do when others approach us is to know they are trying to help, be polite, and protect ourselves from any kind of derailing comment.**

And bottom line: Don't let their own doubt and criticism weaken your potty training efforts. Multiple truths exist in our world...so many seemingly opposing things can be (and are) *true* at the same time. Their opinions, and yours, are not mutually exclusive.

Go forth and let that doubt slide right off your shoulders. It's not yours anyway...it's theirs.

OUTINGS

Always bring a change of clothes with you. Always, always, always. I like to put two dry pairs of undies and pants in the dry part of my wet/dry bag and use the "wet" zippered pocket to stash any wet pants and undies until we get home. (These wet/dry bags are available on my TinyUndies.com store.)

Also always bring a toilet seat reducer of your choice if your child isn't big enough for a regular-sized toilet yet.

I prefer the Potette Plus because you can use it over the grass or concrete as a bottomless mini potty, with the biodegradable bag inserts (found at godiaperfree.com/potettedisposableliners) or with a yogurt container underneath when pottying inside your parked car, with their new reusable liner (found at godiaperfree.com/potetteliner), or, best of all, you can use it as a toilet seat reducer on top of any public toilet. It is incredibly stable, never pinches, and folds up to fit in your bag.

When you arrive somewhere, tell your child where the bathroom is *first*. If she's young and it's her natural time to go, potty her first upon arriving. I always potty my children upon arriving somewhere, especially if the visit involves toys, playtime, or a lengthy grocery stroll. My 14 month old has come to expect it and says "potty" upon parking anywhere, and kindly holds it until we get to the store's bathroom.

When you're in a store, things just get too distracting.

The shopping cart can feel quite similar to a potty for the child who is not paying attention. Also, many children don't realize that places other than home have bathrooms they can pee in. It's helpful to tell him "this store has a bathroom" and to tell him to let you know when he needs to pee and you'll take him there. You can also say, "Tell me peepee if you need to go…and keep your pants dry."

It's also a great idea to bring a mini potty in your car for a while. When you park and have a child who is insisting on pottying, you don't want to be caught without an option.

Either bring a small mini potty, or a duplicate of the one you have at home (if your child has a strong potty preference), or use the Potette Plus that is in your bag. For the super-finicky, carrying a small mini potty like the bEco in your bag (and using it in a public restroom, on the floor) might be necessary until public toilets are accepted.

Also bring a small pack of wet wipes with you, and a cloth wipe. If you have a particularly messy bottom, or goodness gracious, a poop accident, you will be equipped to handle it coolly and calmly.

When out and about, potty first upon arrival, potty last before leaving, and potty anytime you see her peepee dance or she asks to go. Prompt her if it's her natural time (since last she went) or when you get an intuitive thought that it's time to go.

Don't ask, just take, go potty yourself while you're at it, potty older kids too, and then potty your child matter-of- factly. *Time to pee before we shop.*

Bring those Post-It Notes to use over the autoflush sensors as well. Or use a piece of toilet paper laid over top of the sensor while she goes.

You may also want to put a changing pad or PUL- backed pad underneath your child when in the carseat. Kiddopotamus also makes a carseat protector, found at godiaperfree.com/piddlepad. Just in case.

I have to mention that outings usually go much more smoothly than at-home pottying. We parents pay more attention when we're out and about, we are on more of a schedule, and our children are more likely to ask or signal due to the social stigma associated with wetting or soiling in public (it is instinctual to stay dry and clean around others…very instinctual).

PEE ISSUES

Holds it entirely too long. If your child can hold it for a really long time, that is great! Children do not purposely cause pain to themselves, if given the chance. If it hurts, they let it out. So, if your child can drink a ton and wait hours before peeing, she is simply a camel. Some people are just built like that. Get familiar with her pattern and prompt at *her* unique pee interval. And note that some people who hold it this long have to go several times within an hour when they *do* eventually go.

No awareness of having peed. Do some more naked time, Phase 1, Step 1, if your child isn't showing any awareness of having peed.

This is only if she is 100% clueless about it. If she pretends like she didn't pee, or hides it, she *is* aware of having peed. The timeline goes: no clue – oops, I peed – I am peeing right now – I need to pee. If you are certain that you're stuck at "no clue," go back to Phase 1, Step 1.

Pees on the floor when you turn your back. This child is asking for more privacy. Next time it's time, prompt and then leave the bathroom, allowing your naked-bottomed child to finish the deed herself. Otherwise, close the door with the two of you in the bathroom, get him ready to potty (pants down), toss out the prompt, then busy yourself with something else while "ignoring" your child. This provides privacy to the more attached kiddo.

Pees straight through her pants. If you're dealing with a sudden onslaught of accidents after a week or more of pottying success, see "Resistance/Sudden increase in accidents" for information on dealing with this.

If you are dealing with wet pants every day, as the usual mode of operation, here's what to do.

First, you need to teach her how to push her own pants down if you haven't done that already. During a time when she doesn't need to pee, practice this skill so that she has it down-pat when she *does* need to pee.

Dress your child in clothing that he can get down himself, like loose elastic pants or shorts (even those loose Hanes boxer briefs). Your girl can wear loose leggings or pants, or a dress with no underwear. The point is, if a child can't get his clothes off, he will wet right through them.

Second, you may want to **try commando for a few weeks**. The feeling of peeing in pants-only is quite different from peeing in a diaper or underwear. Underwear or trainers may feel too similar to a diaper at first, and for some children wearing them can be an unconscious trigger that it's okay to pee in them. Commando may be your child's magic key…just don't use it for more than 2-4 weeks.

Third, your child may be responding to your prompt "Time to pee" literally, thinking that it's actually time to pee *now*, clothes on. So, you may want to adjust what you say as your prompt, such as *Let's go to the bathroom and get your pants down first*.

Lastly, if your child is just peeing through undies or pants without any warning, and you don't think she's even trying to make it to the potty, there is a gap in knowledge somewhere. Your child may need some more experience in Phase 1, Step 1, where she is learning how to pee on the potty on her own or when prompted, while naked. Once that is mastered and the Step 1 outcomes are reached, move on to the naked at home and clothed outings in Step 2, and then on to Step 3, clothes at home and on outings.

Wearing pants is not an indicator of success, so do not rush to get to the step where she wears clothing. Your child has to get the naked learning down FIRST, and then he can get the pants-wearing down NEXT.

Please also remember to "Be short-winded." If your child knows that the potty is where pee and poop go but keeps peeing on the floor or in his pants, **stop talking so darn much**. She gets it! Speak in simple terms, do not over- explain, and remind her in a really concise manner. *Pee in potty.* And your increased silence will give her more mental room to process what you've said, what she's experienced, and what to do this time and next. It's also a good time to use the toss-out prompt. Prompt her, briefly, and leave the room (or busy yourself with something else).

You may also want to keep the potty in her play area so that she can quickly use it when she needs to go, and gradually move it back into the bathroom. Sometimes the visual reminder of the potty will remind him to leave play and go. See "Interrupting play" for more on that.

Pees all the freaking time. Some children pee every 15-20 minutes because they are experimenting, some because they are bored (taking them to a social setting will encourage them to focus more on interaction and they'll hold it longer), and a small few because of a medical issue such as a UTI (or the warning signs leading up to one).

Yet other children don't finish a full pee when they sit on the potty. They do just a little and hop up and off.

You can encourage pee consolidation by helping your child relax when on the potty, and telling her to flex her belly muscles to be sure she's "pushed" all the pee out, that there is no more pee left in her belly.

You can grunt along with him and encourage him to push those little extra dribbles out. You can count to 3 while doing this. Most kids LOVE to grunt along with their parents and touch their bellies as they contract with the pushing pressure. It is fun.

In all events, pee consolidation does happen naturally, over time, eventually.

You can also encourage longer sitting by using a potty- only toy, singing, running water, busying yourself with something else in the bathroom (with a closed door, both of you in the bathroom together), or "ignoring" him, which in turn gives him more privacy.

If you've got a constant-pee-er, use an egg timer, your iPhone alarm, a potty book, or something else to ensure your child is sitting 2-3 minutes at a time.

See "Won't sit" for more ideas.

Also, try not to rush potty time. Try to encourage getting the business done without doddling, but also give enough time for the bladder to completely empty.

POOP, OVERALL ISSUES

First things first: do not go into potty training fearing the poop part because of whatever you've heard about other parents' potty training experiences.

If you're already pretty deep into potty training and you are having a poop issue, the best advice is to make her feel safe. She can let go, relax, and trust that this is safe...this whole darn thing.

Think about something: How do you typically make your child feel safe in other situations where he is afraid or feels unsafe? Use those same skills in this situation.

Instead of focusing on the fear, feeding the fire, and making it worse, acknowledge, Yes, this is different (not "this is scary")...and this is where you put your poop now. You are safe. It's no biggie.

You also need to stay calm and be a solid foundation for your child. If you freak out about poop, she will too. If you are inwardly freaking out about poop, he will be, too.

One good way to break through your inner poop freak- out is to keep the door open when you are pooping.

Announce, "I need to poop," and go in, leaving the door open. Your child is sure to follow you in there. In fact, we rarely poop alone in our home with a 4 year old and a 14 month old. You get used to it. (And maybe, like me, you long for the day you'll get to use the bathroom completely alone again.) This will help you relax about poop, and in turn your child will see how normal and un-scary it really is.

Consistency and repetition are cure-alls for potty training.

For overall poop issues, be patient, be consistent, and express understanding and empathy during the poop part of potty training. Make this normal for your child.

POOP, MORE SPECIFICALLY

None for the first days of potty training. If everything is going fine with pees in the potty and she is willingly sitting for poop, but nothing has come of it yet, relax and trust that it will eventually happen. If you stay relaxed, and reassure her that it will come, in its own time it will come. A few days of no poop is nothing to be alarmed about. This is hers, after all, and she wants to keep it hers for a little while longer until she feels comfortable. You stay relaxed and consistent and she will feel comfortable to let it out pretty soon.

And, by the way, we adults normally poop only once or twice a day. During potty training, your child will begin to consolidate his poops down to one or two a day, too, as a natural response to having no diaper on. But at first, it's pretty common for there to be no poop for one or two days.

Poops when you turn your back. Your little one just needs a little more privacy. When you turn your back, he's finally got privacy, so he goes! The solution is to bring him to the potty when you see his poopoo dance and to either busy yourself with something else in the bathroom or pretend like you need to get something in the other room. Or sometimes I like to call the dog into the bathroom "Ollie!" and give him attention, which in turn gives my child privacy. Whatever way you can do it, notice when he needs to go and then creatively give privacy so he'll stop pooping when you turn your back…and start pooping when he has privacy and is on the toilet.

Stealth pooping. Kind of similar to the last point, stealth pooping happens with nary a warning signal. At least not one you can consciously detect. The solution to this is to learn her poop timing. If her timing is completely random, then you need to turn the volume up on your poop detecting awareness. Really, really focus on this (again, without her knowing you are focusing on it – ninja-style) and see what is happening during, or right before, pooping. Some children flip to the opposite of what they're doing, or their vibe flips, in the moments before pooping (shifting from stillness to movement, movement to stillness, loud to quiet, quiet to loud, playing interactively to playing independently, being out in the open to hiding behind the couch). Pay attention to these shifts without showing your hyper-attention to him.

Have a mini potty in the living room if your bathroom isn't nearby.

Not making it to the potty in time. This one goes along with the last one. It is truly wonderful that she is trying to get it into the potty! Yay! All you need now is to close the gap by teaching about how that poop comes out. Jamie teaches this one over at Oh Crap. Potty Training and I think it's a great example of how you can teach about poop.

Grab some brown Play-doh and make a fist around it. Tell your child, "When your poop is inside like this, and it wants to come out, tell Mama/Daddy." Then squeeze your fist so the Play-doh comes out of the hole your fingers make, like poop coming out of the anus. "When your poop is here it's too late to tell me…it's already out. So tell me when it's inside (repeat demonstration, Play-doh inside fist) so we can get you to the potty in time. If you wait til it's coming out (squeeze again to demonstrate), then it's too late and we'll have to clean up your poop together."

This demonstration may help fill in the more visual blanks in your child's mind.

Poop on the floor. A couple of times hitting the floor doesn't ruin potty training or your chances of poop training! It's inevitable with some kids, some situations, and very, very common.

You don't want to approve of this by saying "That's okay!" because, in reality, is it OK to regularly poop on the floor? Probably not. Definitely not.

Instead, validate his feelings again and reinforce where it does go…I know this is all new to you and your poop must go in the potty now.

Have your child help you clean up the mess. Usually this is incentive enough to not do it again, but if it happens again, re-state the above and have her help you clean it up.

It's also a good idea to put him on the potty after a poop "miss" because there may be more inside, especially if it's kind of wet or runny. Use your best judgment there.

A very long poo-poo dance. If your child has been doing an obvious poo-poo dance for, say, 7 or 8 hours, and you are worried and really don't want an accident during training, the first thing to do is relax.

Don't pressure your child to sit and poop, or rush the process. Let that full poo-poo dance run its course and reassure your kid that her poop goes in the potty and she can "let go" or "let it slide out" into the potty when it's ready to come out.

Be with her and be reassuring and calming. Once she relaxes, it'll surely come. Any sphincter muscle will only work if relaxed, so work on that, and don't talk too much. See if she prefers to poop on the big toilet or the mini potty (some kids have a preference that they can't quite express).

Then tell her to "let that poop plop into the water…let's listen for it! Then we can look at it." Usually that game is incentive to relax and see what's going to happen.

Now, if your child is freaked out about pooping in the toilet, you wouldn't say that. You'd be a bit more low-key and just work on reading a book together, or relaxing, or say, "Let's sit on the potty so your poop can go where it belongs. Would you like me to sit with you?"

A very intense poo-poo dance. Very briefly (remember "Be short-winded"?) tell her what you see, prompt, and then leave her to it.

I see that you're grabbing your bum and you need to poop. Put it in your potty.

And then walk away and give him some privacy, pretend you forgot something, or just do something else and give him the space to go.

Consistent poop misses. There are a couple of options here. First, I mentioned above having your child help you clean up. It's a good idea to take a good amount of time doing this so that she sees it's no fun to spend all this time cleaning up, but to put the poop in the potty in the first place and move on with playtime.

So, have him help you clean it up, but don't let him dump the poop into the toilet when there's a miss…that is the outcome of getting the poop in the potty: he gets to dump it! If he has a poop accident, clean up is different, and there is no dumping.

Have him get some new underwear and pants, or just pants depending on what you're doing, and help him dress himself.

Another thing you can do is, after a few days where you know she's got the general idea of pottying down, you can (gasp) take a toy away for each ongoing poop miss, because at this point, it is becoming behavioral. If you've never done this before (taken away a toy), you're missing out on a great opportunity to give a negative consequence to an undesirable behavior. A quick, immediate, and relevant consequence does wonders for solving behavioral issues such as laziness.

For instance, if your child throws a toy at you, what do you do? Well, what I recommend is to say, "No, we do not throw toys. Your toy is going in the closet for one hour." No time-out, no scolding, just very clearly stating the boundary and giving an immediate, related consequence.

You have full permission to do this with poop as well, if it is past the point of "she knows what to do" and poop accidents are getting out of hand. No, we stop playing and poop on the potty when we need to poop. Thomas is going into the closet for one hour.

You will not psychologically damage your child by setting boundaries and giving quick, short, related consequences to undesirable behavior.

Remember, someday she will have to follow driving laws, or she will get a ticket as a consequence. He will have to be on time for work or he may be fired from his job as a consequence. These are all life skills, and poop in the potty has now become a requirement in your home.

And it is a reasonable one, don't you think?

If you don't think so, perhaps you are still doubting that you can potty train this early or this quickly or before 3 years of age, or when your child isn't asking you to.

Remember, wait til they're ready is a marketing soundbite. It is simply not true. Then look at the timeline in the history section of this book and remember that only 60 years ago, ALL children were potty trained by 18 months. ALL of them. Poop included. You can do it, too.

Withholding poop / Over 3 days and still no poop. Time to whip out the secret weapons. One is Magic Poop Juice, as Jamie at Oh Crap. Potty Training calls it (Glowacki, 2013). It is a fancy term for your run-of-the-mill mild stool softener, in a toddler-friendly dosage. I also like to use a pouch or two of Just Prunes by Plum Organics, found in most grocery stores, or any kind of prune puree you've got at your fingertips.

We want to encourage that poop to both soften and come out. It will make things easier, because a hard, dormant poop is not going to feel good, or easy, to your child.

So, if you're hitting 3 days of no poop, feel free to do this. With the stool softener, ease in with a half dose, then a half more, and see how that goes. Otherwise, we're talking disaster if you give too much. With the prunes, you really can't overdo it. If 1-2 pouches don't work, try something else.

You can also use a suppository for an immediate poop after a few-too-many days of withholding. They have no side effects and the effects are pretty immediate – between 15-30 minutes and you'll have a poop.

Note: this is different from folks in the early 1900s who used anal suppositories to enforce a pooping schedule. We are not using suppositories to create a mandated schedule.

We are only going to use them if it's been over 3 days and your child needs a little physical help.

If you're potty training a 3 or 4 year old, you may find that a mass of poop forms and only a bit leaks out around it, here and there (pretty common). Use the tools above to soften and release that poop...or see your pediatrician if you need expert help.

So that is it for the poop tools. We want to deal with a poop withheld for more than 2-3 days through the methods above combined with a relaxed attitude on your part.

This will help you avoid a painful eventual poop or a bunch of pee accidents caused by a hard, withheld poop pressing up against the bladder.

So, even though we're gentle parents here, remember, quick and easy is often the gentler choice.

Past issues with the bottom area. If your child has had any medical issues in his life with regards to the anus, colon, or rectum, you will want to take this part of potty training slowly and really have extra compassion (not sobbing sympathy, but expert empathy) for him during the poop training process.

Use the methods described in the last subsection on "Over 3 days and still no poop" to help loosen the bowels and make their passage more comfortable. Your child may remember how painful pooping was if she's dealt with medical constipation or surgery, any type of rectal pain or bloody/uncomfortable stools, in her history. These techniques will help tremendously.

You can get even more creative and cast a magic spell on the potty, transforming it into a soft, easy, happy poo place, with an actual magic wand.

If you'd like to spread a homeopathic balm or your usual natural baby bottom balm around the anus, calling it Magic Poop Balm (again, derived from Jamie's classic potty training terms), you can do that...if your child is okay with that.

Validate her feelings I know it's been hard to poop before, but this (magic poop juice, magic poop balm, magic spell) will make it better.

Seems afraid of pooping. See Fear, pooping in potty.

Stops going mid-poo. He is doing his poo-poo dance or even starts pooping and you transport him to the potty.

Once there, he refuses to finish going.

In this case, you may want to put some books underneath her feet to help her reach that comfortable squat position. You, yourself, should relax, maybe read a book to her, tell her You can do it (grunt along with her if you want)…just let it out.

Create that relaxing and calm environment, and leave the room to get something you "forgot" if you suspect he wants some privacy.

And stay the course. Every time, transport, and eventually things will click into place. See the above poop troubleshooting answers for more ideas.

Skid marks / Fecal soiling (encopresis). If you notice a lot of large "skid marks" or small poop stains on your child's underwear despite good wiping, this is normally due to constipation where poop fluids are leaking out around a ball of hard poop that is trapped in the colon. See constipation for help with this, and if you can't solve the skid marks through solving any constipation, then see your pediatrician to further troubleshoot.

POOP, NIGHT

During the course of potty training, or even a few weeks into this journey, your child's poop timing may have mysteriously changed to "during nap" or "at night"…and you may even suspect that your child is *waiting for the diaper* to poop (if you're still using diapers during sleeptime).

Instead of keeping your child up until you get that poop before nap or bedtime (which can result in *utter* meltdown…you *know* what I mean), **simply ditch the diapers during naptime and nighttime. For good.**

Have your child sleep naked (not commando, not undies, but totally naked) for 1-2 nights (crank up that heat) so that the reminder to wake to pee or poop is much stronger, and the feeling of an accident in bed is aversive enough to prevent future accidents.

The diaper actually *causes* accidents during sleep because it's, again, all she's ever known. IT IS A POTTY. It is there, so she *knows* she can pee or poop in it. If you want her to stop pooping during nap or nighttime, take the diaper away.

During sleep, any type of clothing may feel like a diaper to your child, causing him to unconsciously feel okay with pooping in clothing. That's why you'll do 1-2 days of *stark naked* (at least on the bottom) at night and naps to solve this problem.

By removing the diapers during the night (and naps), she will learn to hold it, she will learn to wake up for it, <u>or</u>, she will adapt by pooping in the potty during waking hours (the last one is the most likely due to the hormones we emit during sleep...they prevent us from soiling ourselves).

See the nighttime/naptime training instructions in Phase 3 for more information and support on accomplishing sleeptime dryness.

PORT-A-POTTIES

Get a Potette Plus (godiaperfree.com/potetteplus). I've said this time and again in this book: this is the best solution for *any* out-of-the-home potty trip. Folded up, it fits in most bags and, unfolded, it fits on top of most toilets, and is incredibly stable. If you don't want to use it in a port-a- potty, simply fold it into a mini potty and use it over the grass or concrete outside of the port-a-potty.

You can also stand your child's feet on either side of the lid or rim and hold him as he squats over the hole. Most kids won't want this adventure, but some will be game. You can also use the EC hold, which is holding her at the thighs with her back against your chest.

Otherwise, bring a mini potty in your car and potty her in there when needed.

POWER STRUGGLES / BACKING OFF

One resource I researched for this book said, "If you and your child have head-to-head battles about toilet training, don't worry. Your child will nearly always win. It's better to wait to demonstrate than to force the issue. Forced toilet training may cause problems later"(Hall, 2014).

Seriously? (And to think I bought this at the local indie bookshop. So disappointing.)

If you let your child win when struggling about potty training, what do you think will happen when your child is a teenager and you're having a power struggle about her curfew? Or drugs? Or sex? Let's think about that.

The better way to handle a power struggle is to let go of your end of the tug of war rope. Don't participate in it.

Back off (which doesn't mean *give up*).

What does this even look like? **Prompt and then walk away.**

Example: She's got her pants off, she's in the bathroom, tell her *Put your pee in the potty*, and walk away. This is how to "back off" without "stopping training."

You stop the power struggle by not pushing the issue while allowing your child to make the right decision on her own, in the absence of pressure or force.

And don't over-talk...if you are a broken record with your child, it will get worse. The power struggle will reach mammoth proportions. Through over-talking, you will be pulling so hard at your end of the rope that she will pull even harder in return. Hand off the power she desires by setting her up for success (pants off) and telling her where to put her pee (direct and short-winded) and then giving her the power and privacy to do it herself.

See also "Resistance."

PRIOR ATTEMPTS AT POTTY TRAINING

If you've attempted potty training before, it's probably been one of two things:

1. You've been really casual about it, very child-led, and there hasn't been any positive ending to the process (you're sitting at mostly- to partially-potty trained, or it's an absolute disaster), or
2. You've waited too long and have now been trying *everything* in order to resolve the situation.

If either of these situations sounds familiar, I have good news. There is hope, and the fixing of previous failed attempts at potty training is relatively simple.

If your child is kind-of potty trained. They are where they are because you have been kind-of-*committed* to potty training. All you have to do is FULLY commit to potty training, stop being "casual" or "gradual" about it, and get serious about doing it (and finishing it).

Go to The Potty Training Plan and directly to Phase 1, and potty train *with 100% commitment* to doing it and completing it. Start to finish.

Remember…ripping the Band-Aid off is much more gentle and much less anxiety-provoking than being casual and gradual.

You did what you did because you *thought* that was the right thing to do. And I don't blame you!! That is where our culture is at…it's not your fault. Just re-commit, and fix it, by doing this plan front to back, once and for all.

Mostly potty trained, totally gets it all, but still wants a diaper to poop in. In this case, stop using diapers at night and do not make them available to poop in (or nap in)…or for anything, even car rides, for that matter. No PullUps, either.

Clear and understandable. If there are no more diapers, there is nothing to struggle against (and nothing to request).

Furthermore, quickly go through all of the steps in Phase 1 and see if there's something that's a trouble area, and then focus on fixing that.

Go through the "Poop" troubleshooting sections and see what you can do there, too.

And know that taking away that beloved diaper that she *needs* to poop in will NOT traumatize her. Nothing in potty training will traumatize her except for strapping her to the potty chair for 7 hours. And you're not doing that, are you?

Make the parental decision, deal with the fallout (however brief it will ultimately be), and move on, warrior.

Remember, if all of a sudden disposables were no longer available on the market, what would you do? What would we all do? We'd deal with the emotional fallout and move on.

Ditch diapers. No going back. No matter what.

Promise? Okay.

Doesn't get it at all. Even though you've tried potty training in the past, perhaps your child does not get it, at all. Yet. Things have not clicked and we can work on that.

If your child is very young, just stay the course…Be steadfast. Remember, just 60 years ago, all kids were done by 18 months. Your child is capable, but you have to make it a priority and stay focused on it. Do not fall into "I'll wait a little longer til she's ready"…remember, *readiness* is a myth.

If your child is much older, she is acting this way because there is a gap in her knowledge. See "Doesn't care."

If you've had a prior potty training attempt DISASTER. You are not the only one! Do not fret. You have not ruined your child. You have not blown all chances of potty training. You are not a terrible parent. There is a ton of hope.

What you will do is a "re-set," which is described below in this troubleshooting section. You will re-diaper and forget about potty training for 2 weeks, then do the Potty Training Plan as outlined in this book.

The reason for this re-set is that *your* nerves are frazzled, and you will be 100% ineffective at toilet training (or anything) while *this* frazzled. The re-set will give you some time to read, review the plan, and get re-centered. It is the perfect amount of time for you to prepare for success.

PUBLIC TOILETS

We are pros at this. As I've done EC with both of my children, we have pottied in 100s of public toilets in several countries over the years, at all ages.

First and foremost, get your child a Potette Plus (godiaperfree.com/potetteplus) and get him or her used to it by introducing it at home on the big toilet. The legs snap into place for use as a mini potty, too, but its biggest benefit is how sturdy it is on all the toilets I've ever tried.

You can also face your child toward the toilet tank and stand her feet at the back of the toilet while you hold her thighs and she's in a deep squat. This could work for poops, but some kids won't like this position.

Also, you can stand your child's feet on the toilet seat and have him stand to pee, boys or girls.

Or, have her place her hands on her knees and bend a little bit forward to get her balance. She will want to hold onto the seat with her hands on either side of her bottom, but germs may freak you out. Either sanitize it first and let her get her balance this way, use the Potette Plus, or have her place her hands on her knees.

To avoid the autoflush going off at an inappropriate time (such as when your child is still *on* the toilet), cover the sensor with a Post-It Note or a piece of toilet paper.

If all else fails, pack the bEcoPotty in your diaper(free) bag and use it on the floor in the public restroom stall like you do at home. In time it won't be necessary any longer.

READINESS QUESTIONS

When things don't go your way, don't happen in 1 or 3 or 5 days to your expectations, or you face power struggles or resistance, you may fall back on the societal crutch of "oh, she's just not ready to potty train yet."

You can totally take this as an "out" and delay potty training. BUT, and this is a big but, training gets HARDER and HARDER at older ages. It just does. So I warn against that, despite what your sister or your MIL says.

Stay the course. I cannot stress this enough. Are you committed or doubtful? Are you distracted or focused? Are you sure you can do this or half-assing it? Be honest…and readjust yourself to get this thing done.

Children are capable of actively participating in pottying (with EC) from birth. Children are capable of wrapping it up and potty training at 18 months, sometimes earlier. 1957…18 months…average age. Remember?

Readiness is a myth. If things aren't going well, breeze through Phase 1 quickly once more and see where there's a problem. Then fix it.

With an older child, he is much more aware of the need for privacy and may resist *more* at the onset of potty training (even at

2 years old, but more commonly with 3 or 4 year olds). Be aware of this and give him more privacy.

You will have less power struggles and less internal wavering regarding whether it's the "right time" to potty train or not if you just go for it and stay the course.

And lastly, don't blame yourself. If you aren't or weren't ready, who cares? You're here now. And you're equipped to do something about it. You can do it.

REGRESSIONS / SETBACKS

I like to call regressions "setbacks" because it's a more accurate term for what a child (and parent) experiences.

Setbacks may occur any time there is a major change or transition in a child's life. Setbacks always pass.

Montessori views a potty learning setback as "a natural temporary reaction to a change in the child's environment" (Seton, 2012).

It is normal and natural. No need to fall down the rabbit hole of despair and start Googling frantically for help. (If you do need encouragement, however, you can get access to our peer support group at godiaperfree.com/ptupgrade and you will get some. Obviously we all need to reach out for support, but random Googling will leave you feeling even more despair.)

Please note: If you *expect* a setback or regression, *you will get one.*

That said, I share these only to help you through them *if* they happen...please do not read these and then *expect* them to occur. Generally, they do not.

If you are getting sudden pee accidents and resistance, and you are not experiencing one of the transitions below, please see "Resistance" for help on this normal part of potty training.

Now for some examples of common causes of potty training setbacks:

- Illness
- Teething
- Moving
- Change in parent's jobs (layoff, new job, working full time again, etc.)

- Divorce
- New baby
- School starting
- You stopped prompting
- Change in potties

If you experience any of the above, the fix is ultimately to work out a solution for the transition that *underlies* the setback. These solutions follow, below:

If it's **illness**, treat the ail and potty training magically gets back on track when the baby is well. In fact, during illness, it's even more important to stay on track with potty training, as catching those diarrheas in the potty is much better for your child and *you*, if you know what I mean.

During illness, a sudden cry or fussiness is often the new pee-pee or poo-poo dance. Be aware of this, as a child with the runs is very uncomfortable right before the poop.

With **teething**, treat the pain with homeopathics or bring out the big guns with Children's Tylenol or Motrin (see packaging for dosage amounts). Remember that children swallow a lot of drool when teething those 2 year molars…and this can come out the other end as diarrhea.

If there's a **big move** coming up, don't delay potty training (if you can help it) and don't revert to diapers if you've already potty trained and are in completion mode. Make it a *priority* to support your child's potty needs during this major transition. (You are going to continue feeding and napping her, yes?) Always tell your child where the potty is and be on top alert for pee-pee dances and integrating transition times during the move, and directly afterward.

Your child needs to feel relaxed and comfortable in order to be potty competent.

So, encourage this in the new environment and reinforce the potty values your child has learned or is learning by being consistent…and take care of yourself during the move by asking

153

for help and taking breaks. My mother always says, "One room at a time. One drawer at a time. One box at a time. It will all get done, eventually."

With a **change in jobs** comes more stress for you and/or your partner. When you are stressed, you lose a handle on other more menial tasks, such as potty learning. Just remember this and continue to prioritize potty training in your household during a change in occupation. You will have to consciously remember to make this a focus of your day. See the "Daycares and caregivers" section for advice on helping the transition to using outside care. And, above all, take care of yourself during this transition.

Regarding **divorce**, please see the sections called "Two homes" and "Single parents." And remember to "Be united" about potty training, as much as you can, through this difficult transition...for your child's sake.

New babies are commonly blamed for potty training regressions in older children. It all comes down to continuing to make pottying one of *your* priorities with your older child (staying consistent in the face of a big change for you as a new-again parent) AND giving adequate attention to your older child so she doesn't vie for your attention through negative methods (peeing on the floor).

Do not *expect* regressions with a new baby. I didn't have one in my house. I didn't expect it. In fact, it was a time of growth for my 3 year old when his new sister came, as he could show her how to potty (we did infant pottying with her from birth) and he could be the big boy role model, too.

Accentuate the fact that your older child can do *so many things* that the baby can't do, because your older one is such a big girl. This makes her feel special and responsible.

And remember...spend some quality alone time with your older child every day, even if it is just his bath and pre- bed book routine, so he has no reason to get your attention in other ways. Have a special date with him out of the house, without the new baby, once a week.

Tend the relationship as best you can, and remember that your own stress and overwhelm (and extreme exhaustion!) with having a new baby, and now two children to care for, can effect potty training only if you lose your commitment to it. Do not re-diaper your older one. Stay the course.

Also, if you are pregnant and think you will potty train your older one *after* the baby is born, think again. You are going to be overwhelmed and under-resourced for a few months with two little ones, and two in diapers is no fun.

Potty train *before* your new baby comes and do *not* expect a regression. Help him be a big boy in preparation for his little sister to come. And finish up before she arrives.

Starting school can be stressful for you, the parent, so, as with all of these transitions, mind your own awareness and continue your usual prompts at transition times. Help your child succeed in staying dry at school by reminding him he needs to ask his teachers to go to the bathroom when he needs to go. It's usually as simple as that.

Setbacks sometimes occur because **you've stopped prompting your child to go**. Please continue prompting until your child is independently getting himself to the potty. Just because you are prompting does not mean she is not potty trained. You must support this process for many months, sometimes, to ensure that it sticks, just as you support reminding her to eat or take a nap. Prompts are helpful reminders, and we all need them sometimes. Please see "Resistance" to learn how to avoid over-prompting.

If you **move your child from the mini potty to the big toilet with a reducer**, and you experience a major setback, you can do one of two things: 1) change back to the mini potty for a few months, or 2) get rid of the mini potty *completely* and tell her it's gone, and she must use the big toilet from now on. My husband did the latter with my then- 3-year-old and after about 3 days, he no longer had fits about it. Here again, making a decision and staying the course could be your solution.

If none of this helps in the face of a major transition- related setback, please see the next section on "Re-setting" and start the process over, anew.

RE-SETTING (STARTING OVER)

If you are completely freaked out by the process and things are not going well, or if you have been trying other potty training methods and it's ended up a disaster, you need a break, my friend.

A re-set is a great time to re-center and take your mind off of potty training for a while so that you can do it more effectively once the period has passed. It's also a nice break for your child and a time period where she can relax back into normal life.

Everybody wins.

How to do it: Mark your calendar for exactly 2 weeks and tell your child "You are going to use diapers again for 2 weeks. If you want to use the potty, just let me know, but otherwise you will use the diaper while we take a break."

And then use the diaper for exactly 2 weeks, no more, no less. ONLY potty your child if she asks directly and you know she's serious (you can tell when your kid is playing around, I bet)…or potty if you see an obvious sign and she usually doesn't resist (like just the poops, or a wake-up pee). But at the minimum, please do not potty at all in order to do a really effective re-set for the both of you.

At the end of 2 weeks, do Phase 1, Steps 1, 2, and 3, with renewed focus and confidence. Ditch the diapers again, anew. Be very calm and matter-of-fact. Be committed, stay the course, and do not waver.

You should only need to do <u>one </u>re-set to be effective.

Do it, enjoy it, and then get serious about potty training and finish that process with renewed energy and focus.

RESISTANCE / SUDDEN INCREASE IN ACCIDENTS

The main reason for 95% of resistance is parental hovering and a hyper-focus on pottying, including over- talking, over-prompting, and underlying anxiety/unintended pressure.

In all cases of sudden resistance and an increase in accidents, your child is asking for more control over this process. Full control.

It's crazy because he's not self-initiating yet and you aren't sure if he can do it himself, especially with all the resistance and accidents. You think you need to stay on him so he can truly integrate everything. *But staying on him is the wrong thing to do.*

For all of these instances, **prompt less often – only prompt when absolutely needed and do it without over- prompting**.

Here's how:

If and when you know it's time for her to go, **casually toss out a reminder to her** and remember to set her up for success...pants are down (if she can do it herself, let her, otherwise, help as needed) and the potty is there...then say *put your pee in the potty* and ignore her, door closed, do something else in the bathroom (if she's somewhat younger), call the dog in and pay attention to him instead, or **just leave, pretending you forgot something in the other room**. *I forgot something – I'll be right back!*

She can now make her own decision and will feel in control of this process, which is what she's asking for with all the sudden resistance and increase in accidents.

This makes it her own, and it's much easier than trying to deal directly with the resistance.

He's not being defiant or difficult...he just wants more control. So give it to him. Take the leap and trust. Be brave. Continue to prompt but in a low-key, make your own decision sort of way. Toss it out there.

Talk about it *only* when needed (time to pee) and remember? Be short-winded. *It's time for you to pee* and leave the room.

This is called "backing off" without giving up or waiting til she's truly ready for potty training (a day which, unfortunately, may never come).

Resistance is NOT a sign that your child is not ready. The longer he stays in diapers, the more the resistance will increase. Putting him back in them will backfire.

Resistance IS a sign that your child is ready to do it himself...with your subtle ninja prompting, of course.

Please see "Accidents" for more information on a sudden increase in accidents.

SINGLE PARENTS

You have it easier, in a way. Whatever your choice about potty training, you get to decide and stick with it without depending on another person to align with.

And…you have more reason to be done with diapers. You have to change them all, and that is no fun.

Please enlist someone, a friend or parent or family member, to help you over the weekend and few days you'll be potty training. Ask someone to come and help cook, clean, and generally support you in this process.

People are much more willing to extend help than we realize (especially to a single mom or dad)…and if you don't ask, they won't have the chance to be your hero or heroine.

Asking for help is a big deal for lots of people (myself included). Do it just this once. Be brave.

SPECIAL NEEDS

Several parents of 0-18 month babies in our Elimination Communication community have reported success with pottying special needs children over the years…incredible success, actually. So, I know from experience that special needs children are *capable* of potty learning, it just looks a little bit different, as does feeding, clothing, bathing, and communicating with these children. Not impossible, just different.

You may need to invest in different supplies than the ones I've listed in this book. Perhaps you need a more supportive potty chair or a higher footstool or handles on the seat reducer, etc.

You will use the same method as listed in this book, but it may take a little more prompting, a little more assisting, a little more patience, a sharper eye for signals, and a little more time to reach the outcomes of each phase.

You may wish to rely more on her natural timing to create a potty routine based on those rhythms, and be extra- tuned-in to her signals as it may take more time to get her situated on the potty.

As with all children, you will need to give brief and specific instructions and hands-on guidance with special needs children. Follow the *ways of being* I listed earlier in this book…they absolutely apply to your situation.

Talk to your pediatrician about any medications your child takes to see if they have any effect (adverse or otherwise) on her peeing and/or pooping functions. If you need to soften her stool to make it more comfortable because her medications cause constipation, please do so with your pediatrician's guidance.

Lastly, your special needs child will thrive from the pride and dignity he learns from being able to potty independently. I encourage you to commit to this as early as whatever age your child is today, and to practice it much like those with younger babies practice EC…a lot more hands-on, a lot more active on the parents' part, and with a lot more patience. It is also priceless to find others with similar children and share successes. Find your support network wherever it may be.

See the "Poop, more specifically, Past issues with the bottom area," section for more information if your child has a history of rectal issues.

SPOUSES AND PARTNERS

In the *ways of being* section of this book we discussed Being United. It's so important for both of you to be on the same page regarding potty training, as children can sense a parental divide and take advantage of it (consciously or unconsciously).

If your spouse doesn't want to be involved with potty training, ask him or her to care for the house, feeding, and cleaning for the weekend while *you* potty train. Allow your partner to help in whatever way she or he chooses, offer much appreciation, and potty train without spite for your spouse's refusal to help.

Chances are, he may feel afraid of failure, she's never done this before, he doesn't want to be the fool, she doesn't want to screw it up. No worries. You handle it and request that s/he take care of the rest while it gets done.

Do not keep diapers in the house once you've begun potty training (except for naps/nighttime until you've done that bit…and hide those). That way, your spouse cannot revert to diapers in a down moment. No diaper…no "easy out."

In time your spouse will see the positive effects of potty training. If s/he wants to dive in and help after some success has been achieved, encourage that, and also encourage him or her to read this book so you both can "Be united."

TANTRUMS

Prompt (remind her it's time to go) and walk away. A tantrum does not continue in a room with no audience!

Make sure there aren't any barriers to success (pants are off, toilet is available, etc.), tell your child *Put your pee in the potty*, and leave the room. The crying will continue only so long as you bear witness to it.

Use this tip for all tantrums, potty or not. Leave the room. If he follows you, leave that room, too. *When you calm down, mommy will talk to you.* No begging, pleading, or bribing.

TRAVEL

I have a ton of personal experience in this as well, and with my readers who've done worldwide traveling, so here are my traveling tips for parents of newly potty-trained kids:

1. **Always locate the potty first.** When entering the airport, a restaurant, or a shop, find the restroom and have everyone, including yourself, potty first (if appropriate), then enjoy what you're there to do.
2. **Bring a small mini potty with you.** Instead of filling your carry-ons with diapers, you can fit a small mini potty into the bag, or the Potette Plus with a package of the biodegradable bags they sell with them (see Supply List). Most airlines allow for a diaper bag as a bonus carry-on

160

(although yours may be a diaper(free) bag!). Use the potty at your seat when that seatbelt sign prevents you from using the lavatory on the plane. Otherwise, use it as a seat reducer in the lavatory.

3. **Pack only what you need.** You'd be surprised…pottying on the road can sometimes be a lot more efficient than it is at home. No one is bored, everyone is in the present moment and connected to immediate needs, things move more smoothly. Bring the minimum of things and know that you can grab extra gear in most places along the way. Just remember that you'll probably be more attuned to your child while traveling, and that misses are normally going to be only pees if you're paying attention and your child is simply adjusting to a new hotel or city. Most children don't have poop accidents in places where they aren't familiar with people or things, or when they're in social situations.

4. **At every new place of lodging, tell your child where the bathroom is FIRST.** Show your child to it, say she can go if she needs to, and generally get settled in. If you've brought your mini potty, set that up near or in the bathroom. Whether at a hotel or in a tiny bungalow, having a little potty station is quite key if that's what your child is used to at home. It translates as portable comfort.

5. **On airplanes, request the bulkhead seats when available.** Especially on a long international flight, you'll appreciate the legroom. It's priceless to have some room to set your potty on the carpet and potty your kiddo there while the (sometimes eternally-on) stay in your seat light is bright. You can usually request these seats when you book your flights. Even airlines that no longer assign seats ahead of time will make an exception for those with small children.

6. **For nighttime/naptime, set up the sleep space like you would at home.** Try to emulate the home night pottying environment as much as possible. Again, pack light, but also try to make things easy and familiar during those wee hours of potty time, if you have a child you who is still waking to pee at night.

7. **Always take your child with you when YOU need to go to the bathroom.** Whether you're at the in-laws or in a restaurant, it's good practice to always bring your child with you and offer. It will help you remember to stay attuned to her needs, and often we need to go at the same time.

8. **For social time at family or friends' homes,** pay attention to how much time has passed and take your child to pee at the usual intervals (based on his natural, usual potty rhythms). Take advantage of transition times, like before or after a meal, to limit disruptions to family activities. Remind your child that she can ask anyone in the home, Grandma, Grandpa, cousin, where the bathroom is when she needs to go. Sometimes our kids don't realize that every home has a toilet and that every person in it is probably willing to help them find it and use it.

9. **Stay consistent, utilize transition times, and stay in tune with your own intuition.** Don't just drop the potty routine because you're on vacay. That is what screws things up when traveling, not the traveling itself. Keep doing your wake up pees, prompting based on natural timing and peepee dances, and your potty-upon-arrival transition time pottying. Pay attention to when that little voice in your head says, "It's time." And also pay attention to when potty paranoia is mistaken for potty intuition…if you're nervous about having a miss in public, be prepared with a potty seat and just stay aware. Plain and simple. Every parent has experienced accidents in public, and the embarrassment is pretty short-lived…and universal.

10. **If you have a bunch of wet ones in a row…remember that you're traveling!** Your child is adjusting to new environments on a more acute level than you are. Don't get frustrated and don't give up. Gather new information from any possible spree of misses and adjust your game. Your potty practice will definitely get back on track when you return home, given you stay consistent and steadfast. Usually misses while traveling indicate that your child is

adjusting to the new environment…no need to freak out about it. Just find ways to make it "home" and press on.

11. **While driving or doing an extended road trip, always potty before getting in the car and at every stop, if appropriate.** Have a potty ready in the car in case you need to pull over. If your child is telling you she needs to go, with words or fusses, or if she just woke up from a nap and is restless, you should pull over and oblige. Protect your carseat with something just in case, but always tend to your newly-potty-trained child's requests to go, continue to pay attention to her natural timing, and offer at transition times (when you are already planning a stop).

12. **Do not regress, yourself.** If you cave in and buy diapers while traveling, you give your child the message that you weren't committed to potty training after all, and he shouldn't be, either. If you presently use sleeptime diapers, continue to use those on your trip. If you have already rounded the potty training corner and are working on independence at this point, proceed as you began. Do not revert to diapers. Whether you realize it or not, traveling with a newly potty trained child is actually easier than our fearful thoughts tell us. We are all more "on it" when on the go…and your child will feel so much pride when you stay on the potty training path while you travel. You can do it. Travel is not a reason to revert to diapers. Rise to the occasion…your child will, too.

TWO HOMES

If you are separated or divorced or co-parenting in two separate homes, I have some tips for making this easier on your child regarding potty training.

First, both of you should ideally read the same book on the topic (feel free to share this book with your ex). Have The Potty Training Experience (Phase 1) occur at one home and the Ongoing Independence (Phase 2) occur at both homes in a similar manner. If you both can be present for the actual training bit, your child will know that you are both in full support of this, and expecting the same results. (If this is impossible for obvious reasons, one of you do the training and the other read about it so you know what has happened, and how best to support it.) Nighttime and naptime training (Phase 3) should happen concurrently as well.

Set up the potty stations in both homes as similarly as possible. Use the same underwear, training pants, or go commando the same way. Encourage similar routines. Share notes and troubleshoot together…for the sake of your child.

Worst-case scenario, I *have* helped parents whose ex's have refused to engage in potty training and would only use diapers when the child was in their care.

The outcome? Their children *insisted* on using the potty at the stubborn parent's house within a very short period of time (a month or two). They outright refused diapers at a certain point. The other parent was then forced to stop using diapers, by the child's insistence.

Also, **if you can't get your ex on-board**, be patient and consistent and potty train anyway, tell him or her what you've accomplished when you're done, and *suggest* she/he use these cotton pants (buy them for him/her) during the child's waking hours. And leave it at that. Don't force, cajole, or guilt them into compliance.

Just give the tools, share the results and how-to's, and leave them to make the good decision.

WIPING

Children can wipe themselves at earlier ages than you would have guessed. As with everything taught in this book, it takes some repetition and consistency for them to learn various parts of the potty routine.

Make wiping a part of the routine, each and every time, and reinforce the learning at every potty visit.

For you moms who may not know, a boy will not have to wipe his penis. A little bounce or shake will do, if you can manage teaching that.

A girl should blot her yoni with a little bit of toilet paper.

With poop, for both boys and girls, it helps to teach them to bend over a little bit while they wipe, as this spreads their cheeks apart a little bit.

If your child has trouble finding her anus, have her do a little exploration in the bathtub sometime. If she can find it in the tub, she can find it when wiping.

Then, boy or girl, have your child grab a little bit of toilet paper and wipe his or her bottom until the paper is clean. If it comes out with a little poop on it, she'll put that in the toilet, grab some more toilet paper, and try again. When it comes out clean, he's done.

If you've got a bit of a messy bottom, keep some baby wipes nearby and have him do the same thing with a wipe. It will be easier to get a really dirty bottom clean with some moisture. Be sure to dry the area right after using a wipe, with some toilet paper or a cloth, to avoid any sort of rash.

You can gradually teach wiping by doing it for her first, then starting it for her and having her finish, or having her start and you finish, and then, lastly, having her do the whole process.

You can always help with wiping as necessary, and for as long as you are fine with it, but remember, your child is capable of much more than you know, or than he'll let on.

With repetition and patient, brief instructions, and a little guiding of hands, your child can learn how to independently wipe poop and pee as early as you teach it.

As an example, my son could independently wipe at a little before 3 years of age, after some focused teaching for about a week, though he continued to claim that he couldn't do it in other situations, with other caregivers, for a while longer until he was 4. It took telling the other caregivers that he *can* do it himself for him to stop whining to them to help him wipe. Kids.

WON'T SIT

This stage will pass, just as some children temporarily resist the high chair, carseat, and being strapped into a stroller or napped in a crib. And, it's very common.

Try to catch your child's attention, and keep it, long enough for him to finish the deed. You want to normalize that your child now sits and pees/poops every time. Do not make a huge pony show of it, but you can do some things, at first, to get him used to sitting.

If your child won't sit at first, read a book, do a song with sign language (we love Twinkle, Twinkle), count to 20 together, or have a fun potty-only toy that she gets only when she sits on the toilet. I'd even go so far as to suggest using your iPhone or iPad in these situations (temporarily). Sit and relax. Those are our goals.

Jamie suggests using a "Calm Jar" that keeps the child's attention long enough to go, and helps avoid the popping- off-and-peeing-2-seconds-later thing that is also very common (Glowacki, 2013). You use a jar or plastic bottle and fill it with medium-sized glitter, oil, and water, and seal it up tight. This will fascinate for many minutes, every time.

Then, over time, you can (and should) reduce the use of these tools to give your child more privacy and to reduce his dependence upon them, as they can become distractions if overused.

More ideas:

Your child may also respond if you tell her *I need to **hear** more pee*, inspiring her to give you something to listen to as opposed to doing something that may seem abstract to her (*finish your pee in the potty*).

You may want to look at what kind of potty or seat reducer you're using. If you have a touch-sensitive child, you may want to invest in a potty cozy to warm the mini potty seat, or use one of the seat reducers I recommend that have soft, cushy padding and characters on them (whether your child watches TV shows or not, the characters are fun to sit on).

Also, consider using a seat reducer instead of a mini potty for the constant escapee. It is a way of trapping them up high. Don't sit or squat too near the toilet when using a seat reducer, as most kids will dive off into your lap and won't learn how to balance on it…or stay put.

Lastly, when you guys go into the bathroom, *close the door* with both of you in it. This way, your child can pop up and down from the potty as many times as she sees fit. It may not make sense to you, but she is practicing and getting comfortable with her potty. Allowing her to pop off and on for a while, but preventing escape by closing the bathroom door, will give her some time to explore this new thing.

In time, she will stop practicing and will sit long enough to go. If you busy yourself with something else in the bathroom while you allow her the space (while naked on the bottom, of course) to explore and pop on and off the potty, she will have room to make the decision of going on the potty herself.

As a last resort, you may want to do what some of my extremely gentle but out-of-ideas readers have done in the past: hold him on it for a few seconds…in a hug.

Remember getting your fussy or finicky baby or toddler buckled into the carseat? On occasion, you probably had to hold her in it and force her to sit while you buckled her up.

It probably only had to happen once, and she probably inwardly appreciated you setting a clear boundary for her. No one got hurt, and even more important, she was safe and secure in your car so she *really* would not get hurt if you got into a wreck.

Same with sitting, at first, with some very physical children. It often helps to hug him onto it and calmly say *this is where your pee goes now, just relax honey.* Use your own discernment with this one. Some think this is force, but if you think it is, what is holding her down in the carseat to get her buckled up? It's for her safety. For some parents, this is the way to set a boundary with a very physical child…gently hugging him on it shows the physical "we sit to potty" lesson, more directly than talking about it, for this kind of child.

One of my most gentle clients potty trained after 2 years of doing elimination communication with her daughter. She wrote of her success, after weeks of resistance with EC:

"By catching the pees when she'd already started to pee a little (Phase 1, Step 1), I made sure she really had to go and then I didn't let her get up from the potty. I knew if it had been more than an hour she'd have SOME pee to push out, so I held her on the potty until she did it. The first time she cried a lot, but then she started to do big pees in the potty every 90 min or so and rarely resists."

So, there you have it. A viable option if you need it.

If you have any questions that were not answered in this Troubleshooting section, please gain access to our private peer-based support group at godiaperfree.com/ptupgrade for more hands-on assistance and support.

REFERENCES

Ambulatory Pediatrics Journal. (2001). Factors Associated With Toilet Training in the 1990s. *Ambulatory Pediatrics , 1* (2), 79-86.

Azrin, N. H., & Foxx, R. M. (1974). *Toilet Training in Less Than a Day.* New York: Pocket Books.

Brazelton, T. B. (1962). A Child-oriented Approach to Toilet Training. *Pediatrics , 29*, 121-128.

Contemporary Pediatrics. (2004). Toilet training: Getting it right the first time. *Contemporary Pediatrics , 21* (3), 105-122.

Glowacki, J. (2013). *oh crap. potty training.* (P. Kirstin Hendrickson, Ed.) Providence: Lovebugs LLC.

Hall, D. J. (2014). *Toilet Time: A training kit for girls/boys.* New York: Barron's Educational Series.

Jaques, R. P. (2012). *That's How I Roll.* Moore, OK: Self.

Lekovic, J. M. (2006). *Diaper-free Before 3.* New York: Three Rivers Press.

NY Times. (1999, August 3). *PERSONAL HEALTH: How to Keep Toilet Training From Being a Power Struggle.* Retrieved November 11, 2014, from NY Times: http://www.nytimes.com/1999/08/03/health/personal- health-how-to-keep-toilet-training-from-being-a-power- struggle.html

Olson, A. (2013). *Go Diaper Free: A Simplified Handbook for Elimination Communication, for babies age 0-18 months* (Vol. 2). Asheville: Go Diaper Free LLC.

Pantley, E. (2007). *The no-cry potty training solution.* New York: McGraw Hill.

Seton, E. (2012). *Child Neuropsychiatry: Toileting.* Los Angeles: Self.

169

THANK YOU…HELP *ANOTHER* MOTHER (OR FATHER) OUT!

Thank you so much for taking the time to read this book and potty train your child with clear, gentle, and direct teaching. I hope it was (or will be) a positive and enriching experience for you and your family.

Please share your thoughts about this book with your friends (moms and dads!) with the links below…every place counts. (I've programmed these links below so you don't have to do a thing but click.)

So many people want to potty train but don't know where to begin. You can help:

To share this on Facebook, visit
godiaperfree.com/PTfacebook.

To pin this on Pinterest, visit
godiaperfree.com/PTpinterest.

To share this on Twitter, visit
godiaperfree.com/PTtwitter.

To leave a review on Amazon, visit
godiaperfree.com/PTamazon.

Thanks again and take care,
Andrea Olson

PS - You can also stay in touch with our community on Facebook at facebook.com/godiaperfreecommunity, Twitter @godiaperfree, Pinterest at pinterest.com/msandreaolson, and Instagram at instagram.com/godiaperfree.

ABOUT THE AUTHOR

Andrea Olson, M.A., earned her Master's degree in Psychology from Pacifica Graduate Institute in Carpinteria, California, in 2007. She earned her certificate in movement-based expressive arts therapy in 2007 and, previously, her Bachelor's degree in Business (Entrepreneurship & Strategic Management) in 2000.

Andrea has a knack for taking life's more complicated topics and whittling them down into an accessible, simple form. The result of this is GoDiaperFree.com where she has become a pioneer in helping mothers and fathers worldwide regain their "potty wisdom" with any age child or baby, through both of her books. .

Prior to her first pregnancy in 2009, she found that a friend's new baby didn't use diapers. Instead the baby peed into the sink. Intrigued (and living in California where everything weird resides), she decided to practice infant potty training with her future baby from birth. Upon doing EC (elimination communication) with her newborn, she found that it was difficult to translate the EC text into actual practice, so she began writing her first book when her son was 5 months old. When he turned 1, her book became available to the masses via her website, EC Simplified, as a DiaperFreeBaby Mentor in San Francisco, California.

Since that time she's worked with 1,000s of parents worldwide helping them start, maintain, troubleshoot, and graduate EC with babies age 0-18 months. She's since created Go Diaper Free, which is a comprehensive community resource for anyone wanting to stop depending on diapers.

Through her hands-on work with the Go Diaper Free community, she's developed cutting edge work in the infant potty training field and has now transferred this knowledge into the conventional *toddler* toilet training world with this, her second, book.

She now offers her exclusive, and affordable, line of tiny baby underwear at TinyUndies.com, for babies and toddlers age 6 months to 5T (and sometimes older, if the bottom is tiny enough). She's also written and published a board book for babies 6 months and up, Tiny Potty, and teaches coaches worldwide to share the message of EC and potty training in her Go Diaper Free Certified Coach Program.

Andrea lives with her husband, three young children, and backyard chickens in lovely Asheville, North Carolina.

Printed in Great Britain
by Amazon